FOREWORD

This manual is issued to prescribe uniform standards for the management and preparation of correspondence and is applicable to all commands and activities of the Department of the Navy.

The following directives and manuals are cancelled:

SECNAVINST 5216.5D of 29 Aug 96
Secretary of the Navy Writing Guide 14 Apr 06

Local supplements to amplify this manual may be issued and inserted as chapter 13. A local supplement shall not contradict or repeat information contained in this manual.

Forward recommended changes to this manual to:

OFFICE OF THE SECRETARY OF THE NAVY
DIRECTOR OF ADMINISTRATION
1000 NAVY PENTAGON ROOM 4D652
WASHINGTON DC 20350-1000

Copies of this manual may be obtained through normal publications channels, Department of the Navy Issuances Web site; or from the Marine Corps Publications Electronic Library Online Web site. This manual is approved for authorized registered users and distribution is unlimited. Authorized registered users may obtain copies of the publications from:

UNDER SECRETARY OF THE NAVY
PUBLICATIONS MANAGEMENT BRANCH
1000 NAVY PENTAGON ROOM 5D773
WASHINGTON DC 20350-1000

Robert O. Work
Under Secretary of the Navy

THIS PAGE INTENTIONALLY LEFT BLANK

TABLE OF CONTENTS

THIS PAGE INTENTIONALLY LEFT BLANK

REFERENCES

REFERENCE	TITLE
NATO Standardization Agreement (STANAG) Number 2066	Format and Abbreviations in NATO Standardization Agreement
SNDL (OPNAVNOTE 5400)	Standard Navy Distribution List
MCO 5216.19	Administration Action (AA) Form (NAVMC 10274, Rev. 3-86)
SECNAVINST 5730.5J	Mission, Function, and Responsibilities of the Office of Legislative Affairs and Procedures for Handling Legislative Affairs and Congressional Relations
EO 9397	Executive Order 9397
MCO 5215.1K	Marine Corps Directives Management Program
GPO Style Manual	U.S. Government Printing Office Style Manual
SECNAV M-5210.1	Department of the Navy Records Management Program
SECNAV M-5210.2	Department of the Navy Standard Subject Identification Code (SSIC) Manual
SECNAV M-5510.36	Department of the Navy Information Security Program Manual
SECNAVINST 5720.42F	Department of the Navy Freedom of Information Act (FOIA)
5 U.S.C. §552a	Privacy Act of 1974
28 U.S.C. §1074	Federal Rules of Evidence
SECNAVINST 5000.37	Provision of the Department of the Navy Documentary Material
SECNAVINST 5239.3B	Department of the Navy Information Assurance Policy
USD P&R Memo	Policy for Digital Signature Functionality and Acceptance, of 12 December 2006
OPNAVINST 5218.7B	Navy Official Mail Management Instructions
DoD Manual 4000.25-6-M	Department of Defense Activity Address Directory (DoDAAD)
SECNAVINST 5211.5E	Department of the Navy Privacy Act (PA) Program
SECNAVINST 5430.7Q	Assignment of Responsibilities and Authorities in the Office of the Secretary of the Navy
MCO P5600.31G	Marine Corps Publications and Printing Regulations

THIS PAGE INTENTIONALLY LEFT BLANK

CHAPTER 1
Correspondence Management

1-1 **Objective and Responsibilities**

1. <u>Objective</u>. To prescribe uniform standards for the management and preparation of correspondence throughout the Department of the Navy (DON).

2. <u>Responsibilities</u>

    a. <u>The Secretary of the Navy (SECNAV)</u> will administer the DON Correspondence Management Program and coordinate proposed changes to this manual with the Chief of Naval Operations (CNO) and the Commandant of the Marine Corps (CMC).

    b. <u>CNO and CMC</u> will administer the Correspondence Management Program within the Navy and Marine Corps, respectively.

    c. <u>Commanding Officers and Heads of Activities</u> will establish a correspondence management program based on the requirements and guidance of this manual and ensure that:

        (1) Correspondence is screened, controlled, reviewed, and answered accordingly.

        (2) Correspondence practices are reviewed periodically to improve products and procedures.

        (3) The most economical communications media and techniques available are used.

        (4) Only essential correspondence is produced.

    d. <u>Administration Officers</u> will:

        (1) Screen incoming correspondence, assign action offices and due dates, and indicate any required concurrences.

        (2) Review outgoing correspondence for correct format and ensure prescribed procedures are followed.

THIS PAGE INTENTIONALLY LEFT BLANK

CHAPTER 2
Correspondence Standards and Procedures

2-1 **Correspondence Standards**

1. General. To a large degree, the image and effectiveness of the DON is portrayed by the tone, quality, and responsiveness of correspondence. Properly written correspondence that clearly and succinctly establishes a position, correctly and completely answers questions, and conveys the right message, all aid in the effective management and operation of the DON. In order to achieve this, correspondence must:

   a. Be neat in appearance, correctly formatted, error free, and grammatically correct. With the use of computers and advanced word processing software, the long-accepted practice of allowing legible "pen and ink" changes to a piece of correspondence is no longer acceptable. All correspondence shall be free of typographical errors and technically correct before it is signed.

   b. Avoid stereotyping men and women based on gender. Use pronouns and titles that are gender neutral.

   c. Do not write unless you must. A conversation in person, by telephone, or by electronic mail (e-mail) often saves two letters - the one you would have written and the other person's response. Conversations are often better than correspondence for working out details. Confirm your conversation with a short memorandum (also referred to as "memo") to the other person or a "Memorandum For The Record" if issues of importance or policy are agreed upon during the conversation.

   d. Always include a point of contact, return telephone number, and e-mail address when your correspondence might prompt a reply or inquiry.

2. North Atlantic Treaty Organization (NATO). When writing to other NATO Forces use the format and abbreviations in NATO Standardization Agreement (STANAG) Number 2066, Layout for Military Correspondence. STANAG Number 2066 is stocked by the Naval Aviation Supply Office (ASO), 5801 Tabor Avenue, Philadelphia, PA 19120-5099.

2-2 **Procedures**

1. Correspondence through Channels

   a. Use the Chain of Command. Follow your chain of command when corresponding on substantive matters such as command decisions, policy issues, and official recommendations.

      (1) Address communications directly to the top official of the organization concerned by title. Show the action office by including the code or person's title in parentheses immediately after the activity's name.

(2) Address correspondence concerning policy, management decisions, or other important matters via the chain of command or those commands, activities, or offices who have cognizance over the subject matter. This keeps intermediate commands informed and allows them to comment or approve as necessary.

(3) A "Via" addressee will always forward official correspondence with an endorsement. The endorsement may be as simple as using the term "forwarded" when no opinion or comment is needed. A "Via" addressee may elect to take final action, divert the routing, or return the correspondence to the originator with appropriate explanation (chapter 9).

(4) When there is no time to send important correspondence "Via" the chain of command and still meet a deadline, you may:

(a) Send correspondence via the chain of command, with an advance copy to the "To" addressee. To alert all addressees to this unusual routing, repeat the action addressee by Standard Navy Distribution List (SNDL) short title in a "Copy to:" line and include the term "(advance)" after the short title.

```
EXAMPLE:

Copy to:
CNO (advance)
JAG
```

(b) Send correspondence directly to the "To" addressee with a concurrent copy to each intermediate addressee. Include in the text a statement like this: "A copy of this correspondence has been mailed directly to all addressees. Request "Via" addressees forward your endorsements directly to...." Additionally, include the "Via" addressees by SNDL short titles in the "Copy to:" line.

b. Variations to Corresponding Through the Chain of Command

(1) Authorized subordinates of different activities may correspond directly with each other on routine matters.

(2) List any cognizant addressees in the "Via:" line when it is determined that they should see a letter before it reaches the "to" addressee.

(3) Include intermediate commands as "Copy to" addressees instead of "Via" addressees if you want them to see certain routine correspondence without having to endorse it.

(4) Bypass intermediate commands that clearly have no interest in a letter's content and no requirement to comment or act.

c. Individuals Writing to Higher Authority

(1) Navy Personnel. When writing to higher authority on a personal matter affecting the command, prepare your letter on plain bond paper in standard letter format. Examples include requests for retirement or resignation. Address the letter to the higher authority and send it "Via" your chain of command. Each "Via" addressee will prepare an endorsement and forward the correspondence to the next addressee.

(2) Marine Corps Personnel. Use NAVMC 10274, Administrative Action (AA) Form, as prescribed in Marine Corps Order 5216.19 (MCO 5216.19).

2. Take Advantage of Correspondence Shortcuts

a. Facsimile Machines. Facsimile machines provide a fast and reliable means for sending official correspondence (chapter 5).

b. E-mail. You can use e-mail for formal and informal correspondence. See chapter 4 for additional information.

c. Window Envelopes. Window envelopes eliminate the cost of addressing envelopes and the risk of putting letters in the wrong envelopes. To format letters for use with window envelopes see page 7-18. It should be noted that the window-envelope letter format has no "From:" line, so every copy that goes outside your activity must be on letterhead to show its origin. Do not use a window envelope for material that:

(1) Is classified.

(2) Involves national security.

(3) Is of a personal nature.

(4) Is sent to high-level officials.

d. Form and Guide Letters. Periodically review correspondence for recurring, routine topics that can be addressed with a standard response. This standard response can be developed into a form or format letter to save time. See "Form and Guide Letters, an Information Resources Management Handbook by the General Services Administration (GSA)." This handbook is available through the Military Standard Requisitioning and Issue Procedures (MILSTRIP) system.

(1) Use form letters when possible for routine matters that require no personal touch. Avoid form letters when expressing sympathy, apology, or appreciation.

(2) Guide letters are pre-drafted standard letters that contain paragraphs that you may pick from to best fit the situation for which you are writing. Type or print them individually so they seem personally composed.

3. <u>Coordination</u>. Coordination is a critical step in the processing of outgoing correspondence. In order to ensure that a proper response or original letter is prepared, the originator will need to decide who needs to concur before the letter is signed. The originator will obtain appropriate concurrences, resolve major differences, and arrange for any needed retyping.

a. Always coordinate during the drafting stage, before the correspondence is put into final form and submitted for signature. Ensure all coordination inputs are retained and filed with the file copy of the signed correspondence.

b. Limit reviews to only those offices that have a substantial interest in the topic of the correspondence.

c. In some cases, coordination can be done quickly and informally. Discussions by phone or in person or coordination via e-mail are often more efficient than formal written coordination, especially if a letter is brief and routine.

4. <u>Submit Finished Products for Signature</u>. Normally, submit correspondence for signature in final form. Use double-spaced drafts only when changes are likely, perhaps because a subject is controversial or a policy statement needs precise wording. Early guidance to writers about a signer's preferences will reduce the frequency of changes.

5. <u>Signature Authority</u>. Delegate signature authority to the lowest legal and practical level.

a. <u>What the Commander/Commanding Officer/Officer in Charge Must Sign</u>. The commander/commanding officer/officer in charge must personally sign documents that:

(1) Establish policy.

(2) Center on the command's mission or efficiency and are addressed to higher authority.

(3) Deal with certain aspects of military justice.

(4) Are required by law or regulation.

b. <u>Delegation of Signature Authority</u>

(1) Delegation of signature authority may be made to military and civilian subordinates. All delegations of signature authority will be made in writing and signed by the person delegating the authority. If the delegation of authority is provided for in a directive, indicate this delegation in a generic reference to a billet or position title. For each individual that the delegation of authority applies, a letter so delegating that authority to the individual, by name,

will be prepared. Include a brief outline of the scope of delegation, and if appropriate, authorize the individual to further delegate or sub-delegate the authority. In the absence of specific sub-delegation guidance, delegated signature authority shall not be sub-delegated.

(2) An individual who signs correspondence under delegated authority will use the term "By direction" typed below their name when signing documents under this delegated authority.

EXAMPLE: I. M. FRUSTER
                                          By direction

c. <u>Acting for the Commander/Commanding Officer/Officer in Charge</u>. In the absence of the commander/commanding officer/officer in charge, and where specifically authorized by law or regulation, an officer who temporarily succeeds to command shall sign official correspondence with the term "Acting" typed below their name.

EXAMPLE: J. CANNON
                                          Acting

d. <u>Acting for an Official Who Signs by Title</u>. When the signatory has been formally, but temporarily, appointed to replace an official who signs correspondence by title rather than "By direction," the word "Acting" is typed below the typed name.

EXAMPLE: J. IVES
                                          Deputy
                                          Acting

e. <u>Signing "For" an Absent Official</u>. When a piece of correspondence is in final form and the official that would normally sign the correspondence is unable to do so, it is permissible to have the correspondence signed "for." Rather than modifying the document to replace the signature line, an individual already delegated signature authority may sign the correspondence and hand write the term "for" before the typed name of the regular signing official. This method should be used only when a delay would fail to meet a crucial deadline.

6. <u>Signature Stamps/Electronic Signatures</u>. Commanders/commanding officers/officers in charge or civilian equivalents may authorize the use of a signature stamp or an electronic signature that replicates his or her signature where personal signing of a piece of correspondence is impractical or the correspondence is of a routine nature. Personnel authorized to use a signature stamp of someone else's signature shall pen their initials next to each signature they stamp to authenticate the stamp. Safeguard signature stamps from unauthorized use.

7. <u>Incoming Correspondence Controls</u>. Controlled correspondence is correspondence that requires some type of action, requires a response, or has long-term reference value.

a. <u>Date Stamp</u>. Date stamp all incoming controlled correspondence on the day it arrives at the command. It is a good practice to date stamp all incoming correspondence, not just controlled correspondence.

b. <u>Restrict Assignment of Controls</u>. Assign controls to only incoming mail that requires a response or has long-term reference value. Incoming action correspondence should be routed directly from the correspondence management office to the action office. If necessary, send duplicate copies to intermediate or coordinating offices.

c. <u>Track Correspondence</u>. Use OPNAV 5211/7 Correspondence/Document Control Card to track the status of controlled correspondence routed for action.

8. <u>Replies to Correspondence</u>

a. <u>Controlled Correspondence</u>. Take prompt action on incoming correspondence that requires action or a response. Normally, correspondence should be answered within 10 working days or as prescribed by the immediate superior in command or by the tasking authority for the response.

b. <u>Congressional Correspondence</u>

(1) Reply directly to members of Congress if they contact your activity on routine and non-policy matters. When doubt exists over whether to release certain information, contact the Office of Legislative Affairs for guidance.

(2) Correspondence from Congress shall be answered within 5 workdays of receipt. If a response cannot be provided within 5 days, send an interim response that acknowledges receipt of the correspondence and provides an estimated date when a final response will be sent. Send the original response plus an additional copy when responding to a Congressional inquiry. Also, send a blind copy of your final reply and substantive interim replies to:

CHIEF OF LEGISLATIVE AFFAIRS
NAVY DEPARTMENT
WASHINGTON DC 20350-1000

(3) The opening line in the text of the response should read, "Thank you for your letter of [date], concerning [issue]." NOTE: The date format is month day, year (i.e., June 19, 2009).

(4) When responding to a Congressional request, the closing line in the text of the response should read, "If I may be of any further assistance, please let me know."

(5) For more information on the handling of naval legislative affairs refer to SECNAVINST 5730.5J, Mission, Function, and Responsibilities of the Office of Legislative Affairs and Procedures for Handling Legislative Affairs and Congressional Relations.

c. <u>Freedom of Information and Privacy Act Requests</u>. Answer Freedom of Information Act (FOIA) requests and Privacy Act requests within 10 workdays of receipt. If a response cannot be provided within 10 days, send an interim response that acknowledges receipt of the correspondence and provides an estimated date when a final response will be sent. Ensure all responses for FOIA information and Privacy Act information is reviewed by the base or command FOIA and Privacy Act coordinator or the base or command judge advocate general.

9.   Outgoing Correspondence Controls

    a.   Impose Realistic Due Dates. When sending correspondence that requires a response or has action for the recipient, put a "reply by" due date in your letter only when you have a compelling reason to receive a response back by that date. When choosing the due date, allow time for your letter to make its way up the chain of command to be signed, time for it to reach the people who will take action, time for them to gather information and prepare a response, and time for the response to make it back to you.

    b.   Sign and Mail. Correspondence should be signed at intervals throughout the day. This method will keep signed correspondence from lingering overnight before it goes out. Arrange for a special trip to the mailroom for important correspondence that is signed after the last regular messenger and before the last mail dispatch. Alert the mailroom to the urgency.

    c.   Trace Late Replies. If a response is not received within a reasonable amount of time or by the directed "reply by" date, follow up with the command that the correspondence was sent to. There are two methods to follow up on late correspondence:

        (1)   Forward a copy of the original correspondence with the term "TRACER – [date]" written or stamped in the top margin.

        (2)   Contact the command that the correspondence was originally sent to by phone or via e-mail.

10.   Limit Use of Social Security Numbers (SSN)

    a.   Corresponding Within the Department of Defense (DoD). Limit the use of the SSN of a Service member or civilian employee of the DoD unless essential for identification and authorized for use by authority of Executive Order 9397.

    b.   Corresponding Outside of the DoD. Never use or provide the SSN of a Service member or civilian employee of the DoD when corresponding with an individual or agency outside of the DoD. The only exception to this policy is if the individual involved gives written permission to release his or her SSN, or the incoming correspondence you are responding to includes the individual's SSN.

11.   Identifying Navy and Marine Corps Personnel. This information is generally included in the subject line of the standard letter and in the first paragraph of the business letter. Fully identify the member when you first mention him or her. In later references to the member, simply use the rank or rate and last name. Do not capitalize every letter of a member's last name, except in the subject and signature lines. Capitalize the words "Sailor," "Marine" and "Service member" when referring to members of the U.S. Navy or U.S. Marine Corps.

a. <u>Navy Requirements</u>

(1) Abbreviated rank for officers and rate and warfare designator for enlisted personnel (e.g., AD1(AW), BM2(SW), CSSN(SS)) with no space between rank/rate and warfare designator,

(2) first name, middle initial if any, and last name,

(3) staff corps abbreviation (if any),

(4) branch of service,

(5) the last four digits of the SSN, and

(6) the designator for an officer.

```
EXAMPLE:        RADM Michelle L. Howard, USN, XXX-XX-1234/1110
                CDR Gilbert L. Williams, USN, XXX-XX-1234/6410
                LCDR Sean L. Bartlett, SC, USNR, XXX-XX-1234/3100
                MC2 Kevin O'Brien, USN, XXX-XX-1234
```

b. <u>Marine Corps Requirements</u>

(1) Unabbreviated grade,

(2) first name, middle initial if any, and last name,

(3) the last four digits of the SSN without hyphens,

(4) military occupational specialty, and

(5) branch of service.

```
EXAMPLES:       Major Mary J. Smith XXX XX 1234/0430 USMC
                Captain Brent R. Sowders XXX XX 1234/0202 USMCR
                Sergeant Lauren M. Ferrell XXX XX 1234/0411 USMC
```

12. <u>Letterhead Stationery</u>. The standard size paper for all official letterhead stationery is 8-1/2 inches by 11 inches. Preprinted or computer generated letterhead is acceptable. Use white, plain bond paper. Refer to appendix C for stationery usage guidelines.

a. <u>Use of Letterhead Stationery</u>

(1) Use command letterhead stationery only for official matters of the command. Printing names of officials on letterhead stationery is prohibited. When using letterhead

stationery, the "From:" line will always contain the title of the activity head and command name. The "From:" line will never contain the name of an individual.

(2) Use command letterhead stationery when corresponding as a member of a DON approved board or committee. Indicate the letter is from the signing official by using the board or committee title in the "From:" line.

(3) Do not use letterhead as personal stationery. For example, CDR Baker, captain of the ship's basketball team, may not use it for matters involving the team.

(4) The use of letterhead is authorized for commanders, commanding officers, officer's in charge and directors or those who have signature authority for commands that are represented in the SNDL.

b. Letterhead Format

(1) Letterhead stationery of the DON shall bear a one-inch in diameter seal of the DoD. Other seals, emblems, insignia, decorative or emblematic devices shall not be incorporated. See appendix C for additional guidance.

(2) The letterhead begins with "DEPARTMENT OF THE NAVY" centered on the fourth line from the top of the page. Center the activity's name, address, and nine-digit zip code on succeeding lines. Do not use abbreviations or punctuation in the address.

EXAMPLE:

DEPARTMENT OF THE NAVY
CHIEF OF NAVAL OPERATIONS
2000 NAVY PENTAGON
WASHINGTON DC 20350-2000

DEPARTMENT OF THE NAVY
HEADQUARTERS UNITED STATES MARINE CORPS
3000 MARINE CORPS PENTAGON
WASHINGTON DC 20350-3000

(3) The address lines of letterhead for Navy activities shall conform to the SNDL address for that activity. Marine Corps activities shall comply with current Marine Corps Directives Management Program, MCO 5215.1K.

13. Enclosures. An enclosure can prevent a letter from becoming too detailed. Try to keep letters short, down to one page whenever possible, and use enclosures for lengthy explanations that cannot be avoided. An enclosure may include such things as manuals, publications, photocopies of correspondence, charts, etc.

a. Marking Enclosures. Enclosures must be marked on the first page; however, you may mark all pages. An enclosure marking goes in the lower right corner, whether the text is arranged normally or lengthwise. Type "Enclosure" and its number in parentheses. You may use pencil so an addressee can remove the marking easily should the enclosure be needed for some later purpose. Arrange the typed pages lengthwise so they can be read from the right.

EXAMPLE: (First page. The enclosure line is right justified.)

                                                                Enclosure (1)

EXAMPLE: (Succeeding pages. The enclosure line is right justified and the page number is centered and 2 lines below the enclosure line.

                                                                Enclosure (1)

                                    2

   b.   Numbering Pages of Enclosures. Number only second and later pages. If you have several different enclosures, number the pages of each independently.

   c.   Sending Enclosures Separately. When size, weight, or other factors prevent sending an enclosure with a letter, send it separately and type "(sep cover)" after the enclosure's description.

EXAMPLE: Encl: (1) SECNAV M-5216.5 (sep cover)

14. Copies. Keep in mind the following when reproducing paper copies:

   a.   Use two-sided photocopying whenever possible.

   b.   If your letter must have "Copy to" addressees, include only those with a genuine need to know. Be realistic.

   c.   Avoid "just in case" copies and whole batches of 10 or 15 copies when you can pinpoint the quantity precisely.

   d.   Make the most of the "read, initial, and date" approach to information copies within your command. Circulate a single copy among those who need to read the document, and have them pass it on.

   e.   Distribute copies by e-mail or put information copies on your local area network. If using either of these two methods, distribute the copy in approved FAM software application format.

   f.   Avoid redundant file copies. Keep official command files in one central location to simplify access. Retain one official file copy of all outgoing correspondence.

15. <u>Expressing Military Time</u>. Express military time in four digits based on the 24-hour clock. The time range is 0001 to 2400. The first two digits are the hour after midnight and the last two digits are the minutes. Do not use a colon to separate the hour from the minutes.

```
EXAMPLE:   6:30 am in civilian time is 0630 in military time
           3:45 pm in civilian time is 1545 in military time
```

16. <u>Expressing Dates</u>. There are three date formats allowed for use in Navy correspondence. The formats and their use are described below. In all date formats, the day is represented as one or two digits (do not use a zero preceding the numerals 1 through 9 when the day is single digit). The abbreviated format and the standard format are used when corresponding with other military organizations. The civilian format is used when corresponding with Congress, civilian agencies and businesses, and individuals.

    a.   <u>Abbreviated Format</u>. The abbreviated format is only used as part of the sender's symbol, or in the absence of the sender's symbol, as the date for the letter. The format consists of a 1- or 2-digit day, the 3-letter abbreviation for the month, and the 2-digit abbreviated year.

```
EXAMPLE:   1 Feb 09
           25 Mar 09
```

    b.   <u>Standard Format</u>. The standard format is only used in the text of correspondence. The format consists of a 1- or 2-digit day, the spelled out month, and the 4-digit year.

```
EXAMPLE:   5 April 2009
           17 November 2009
```

    c.   <u>Civilian Format</u>. The civilian format is used as both the date of the correspondence and in the text. Do not use an abbreviated civilian format. The format consists of the spelled out month, the 1- or 2-digit day, a comma, and the 4-digit year.

```
EXAMPLE:   May 5, 2009
           December 25, 2009
```

17. <u>Abbreviations and Acronyms</u>. Abbreviations and acronyms are one of the most misused aspects of correspondence. When using abbreviations and acronyms the writer must consider the audience. What is familiar to you may not be familiar to the reader. The use of abbreviations and acronyms tends to detract from the content of the correspondence by causing the reader to have to pause, remember what the abbreviation or acronym means, then continue reading.

    a.   Established abbreviations are acceptable in all but the most formal writing (e.g., directives). Some examples include "Mr." (Mister), "Ms." (Miss), "e.g". (for example), "i.e." (that is), and "etc." (et cetera), "sonar" (sound navigation and ranging), and "radar" (radio detecting and ranging).

    b.   Do not abbreviate military titles in the text of press reports.

c. If you use an acronym, spell it out first and then define the acronym in parentheses. After the initial definition, the acronym may be used without explanation.

EXAMPLE: North Atlantic Treaty Organization (NATO)

SECOND USE: The NATO is holding a meeting in March.

18. <u>Punctuating, Capitalizing, Spelling, Hyphenation, and Separating Words</u>. For examples on punctuating, capitalizing, and spelling, refer to the Government Printing Office (GPO) Style Manual. Most word processors eliminate the need to divide words. If correspondence is produced manually, use the Word Division Book, a supplement to the GPO Style Manual or your dictionary for help with dividing words. Use hyphens sparingly; a slightly uneven right margin is preferred over hyphenated words. Never hyphenate a word at the end of a page. Avoid separating words in close association such as a person's name, abbreviated titles, and dates. If a full name must be split, do so after the first name, when there is no initial, or after the initial. Never split the name of a ship.

19. <u>Proofreading</u>. Proofread correspondence several times and check it carefully to ensure it has been correctly prepared. A recommended method of proofreading is:

a. Check format first. Do not read for substance until you are sure everything else is right.

b. Look at the framework of the correspondence:

(1) Is letterhead correct/straight?

(2) Are the margins 1 inch?

(3) Are page numbers centered 1/2 inch from the bottom of the page?

(4) Is there enough/too much room for the date?

(5) Are paragraphs aligned/indented properly?

(6) Are paragraphs sequentially numbered/lettered?

(7) Are enclosure markings correct?

(8) Are more than three lines hyphenated, and are successive lines hyphenated?

(9) Is there enough room for the signature line?

c. Next, look for typographical errors, misspelled words, improper punctuation, improper spacing, and incorrect grammar:

(1) Read slowly. Look at each word separately.

(2) Look up all hyphenated words you are not sure of.

(3) When using a word processing program, use spell check and grammar check; however, never solely depend on this method. Utilize spell check and grammar check as an additional tool.

d. Lastly, read for content.

20. <u>Typeface</u>. For text, use 10 to 12 point font size. Courier New 12-point is the preferred font style and size for official correspondence (e.g., directives), but fonts like Arial, Times New Roman or CG Times may be used for informal correspondence. Bold, underline, script, and italics may be used for occasional emphasis, but not for entire letters.

21. <u>Color of Ink</u>. Only use black or blue-black ink to sign correspondence. Photocopiers pick up these colors well.

THIS PAGE INTENTIONALLY LEFT BLANK

CHAPTER 3
Electronic Records

3-1 **General**. An electronic record is any information that is recorded in a form that only a computer can process and that satisfies the definition of a Federal record (SECNAV M-5210.1 Department of the Navy Records Management Manual, part I, paragraph 17) -- information made or received in connection with the transaction of public business and preserved or appropriate for presentation as evidence of the organization, functions, policies, decisions, operations, etc, or because of its information value. Electronic documents, including e-mails, are Federal records to the same extent as their paper counterparts would be. In practice, there is no difference between managing electronic and paper records.

3-2 **Procedures**

1. Creation. Before a document is created on an electronic records system that will maintain the official file copy, each document must be identified sufficiently to enable authorized personnel to retrieve, protect, and dispose of it. When feasible, create the electronic record within a DoD certified electronic records management application (RMA), such as Hewlett Packard Total Records Information Management (TRIM) Context, using procedures established for record creation within the RMA.

    a. Naming Files. Naming electronic files resembles labeling paper file folders. When naming subdirectories or "folders," use the Standard Subject Identification Code (SSIC) (SECNAV M-5210.2, Department of the Navy Standard Subject Identification Code (SSIC) Manual) and any logical combination of alphanumeric characters permitted by the operating system and descriptive of the series. For example, a subdirectory labeled 5240 would show "General Administration and Management" files containing correspondence on industrial methods that are destroyed after 5 years. Identifying information for each document may include the office of origin, the SSIC, key words for retrieval, addressee (if any), signature, originator, date, authorized disposition (coded or otherwise), and security classification (if applicable). Ensure that electronically maintained records can be correlated with related records on paper, microform, or other media. When creating within, or transferring to, an approved RMA, comply with specific naming, identification and tracking requirements established for the RMA.

    b. Labeling Disks or Tapes. Adhere to the following procedures when it is not practicable to create or maintain an electronic record within an approved RMA (for example, none is available to the activity). To prevent damage to the disk or tape, write the information on the label before you put it on the disk. Never erase information on a label once it is in place. When affixing a label to a disk, choose an area away from all holes. Be sure labels identify the hardware and software that will read the information, security classification (if applicable), the SSIC, description, and disposition instructions. Do not affix external labels to Compact Disk – Read Only Memory disks.

2. <u>Maintenance</u>

a.   Electronic records that are not created within an approved RMA should be transferred to one as soon as practicable within 6 months of the record creation date. However, electronic records whose disposition schedule permits destruction within 6 months of the date the record was created need not be transferred to, or maintained within, an approved RMA if destroyed within that 6-month period. Once an electronic record is within an approved RMA, adhere to the maintenance requirements established for that RMA. Pending transfer into an approved RMA, or when an approved RMA is not available, adhere to the procedures in paragraphs 2b through 2d below to protect electronic records.

b.   Make backup copies of files at least once a week. Do not use floppy disks for long-term storage of permanent or unscheduled records because floppy disks are vulnerable to mishandling and data loss is common. When disks are the only backup medium available, use them for temporary storage only. If possible, store the backup media in a separate area from the source data to provide additional insurance against data loss. As noted in the preceding paragraph, these backup procedures are not required for an electronic record maintained in an approved RMA.

c.   Equipment failure and power outages are additional causes of data loss. Save files frequently. When using a word processing program, set the auto save feature to every 5 minutes.

d.   Store frequently used files conveniently for immediate access. Store less frequently used files on tape, disk, or other media.

e.   Manage, use, and delete classified information under the guidelines contained in SECNAV M-5510.36, Department of the Navy Information Security Program. Be sure the records you maintain are necessary and pertinent. Appropriately destroy non-essential records.

3. <u>Restrictions</u>

a.   <u>FOIA</u>. TheFOIA allows any person to seek access to records held by a Government agency. See SECNAVINST 5720.42F, Department of the Navy Freedom of Information Act (FOIA),, for information on processing requests.

b.   <u>Privacy Act</u>. The purpose of the Privacy Act of 1974 (5 U.S.C. §552a) is to balance the Government's need to maintain information about individuals with the rights of individuals to be protected against unwarranted invasion of their privacy stemming from Federal agencies' collection, maintenance, use, and disclosure of personal information about them. As such, limit access to personal data and other restricted documents.

. c.   <u>Electronic Records as Evidence</u>. Under the Federal Rules of Evidence (28 U.S.C. §1074), electronic records are acceptable to the courts as evidence; however, each judge is free to dismiss evidence on the basis of the court's independent evaluation.

4. <u>Disposition</u>

a. Identify and schedule electronic versions of official records for disposition. Refer to SECNAV M-5210.1.

b. Erase electronic files used only as backup files or that only contain passing information once a hard copy has been generated or when the data is no longer needed.

THIS PAGE INTENTIONALLY LEFT BLANK

CHAPTER 4
Electronic Mail

4-1 **General**. E-mail lets individuals and activities exchange information by computer. You may use it for informal communications in place of telephone calls or to transmit formal correspondence. The Defense Data Network must be used for long-haul data communications support, unless the host system is waived. Whatever you send by e-mail must be for official Government business or for authorized purposes (as defined by the Joint Ethics Regulations section 2-301 (DoD 5500.7-R)). E-mails are subject to legal discovery, therefore, care should be taken to ensure e-mails are created and managed appropriately per SECNAVINST 5000.37.

4-2 **Procedures**

1. Managing E-mail. Activities will establish procedures for accessing and managing e-mail. Among other things, they must:

    a. Prohibit users from sharing mailboxes or passwords.

    b. Encourage users to check their mailboxes frequently, but at least twice a day.

    c. If you are absent for more than 3 days, ensure you annotate that in your automated e-mail response. Provide a point of contact for e-mails requiring immediate response.

    d. Provide for periodic review of e-mail files to purge, retain, or file as appropriate.

2. Formal Correspondence. Activity heads may authorize the use of e-mail to correspond formally. Your delegation of signature authority for correspondence is also your release authority for e-mail. When corresponding formally:

    a. Use standard DON correspondence formats including an SSIC, serial number, date, and signature authority.

    b. Type in your letterhead information to identify the originating organization.

    c. Use "/s/" in place of the signature.

```
EXAMPLE:                          /s/
                                  C. PALMERONE
                                  By direction
```

    d. Follow your chain of command.

    e. Transmit only from your authorized e-mail address.

    f. Request acknowledgement of receipt in the original communication when it is required. Acknowledgement may be via e-mail.

g.   Keep a copy of any formal correspondence sent by e-mail as your activity's file copy (see paragraph 5 below).

3.   <u>Informal Correspondence</u>. There are no specific guidelines for informal correspondence; however, keep it brief, use good taste, and observe traditional customs and courtesies. Do not use a complete signature line to identify the sender, but the sender must be fully identified. You may omit the signature line entirely if your computer automatically identifies the sender.

4.   <u>Security and Privacy Issues</u>

a.   Do not send classified information by e-mail unless the system, including the network, is protected for the highest level of classified information you are sending. Refer to SECNAVINST 5239.3B,, Department of the Navy Information Assurance Policy, for additional guidance on automated information system security.

b.   Follow established guidelines and exercise good judgment in transmitting sensitive information such as:

(1) Government information that would be of value to an adversary.

(2) Pre-award contractual information, budget information, or authorization data.

(3) Non-government information such as trade secrets the Government agreed to keep confidential.

(4) "For Official Use Only" information.

(5) Information governed by the Privacy Act of 1974.

5.   <u>Records Management</u>. E-mail lacks the built-in records management controls of the Naval Computer and Telecommunications System (NCTS) and the Automatic Digital Network (AUTODIN). An e-mail can be considered a record (see chapter 3, section 3-1, of this manual for the definition of an electronic record). Activities will control the creation, use, maintenance, and disposition of e-mail records. Follow chapter 3 of this manual and SECNAV M-5210.1.

6.   <u>Digital Signatures</u>. DON policy for digital signatures continues to evolve. However, two uses of digital signature have been established. In accordance with SECNAVINST 5239.3B, commanders of DON organizations shall ensure e-mail messages requiring either message integrity or non-repudiation are digitally signed using DoD Public Key Infrastructure (PKI). All e-mail containing an attachment or embedded active content must be digitally signed. Per DoD guidance (USD P&R Memo, Policy for Digital Signature Functionality and Acceptance, of 12 December 2006), digital signatures will be recognized and accepted as valid for all human resource management documents.

CHAPTER 5
Facsimile Transmission Services

5-1 General. Facsimile machines provide a rapid and reliable alternative to the various mail systems for the transmission of documents. Whatever you send by facsimile must be for official Government business or for authorized purposes (as defined by the Joint Ethics Regulations section 2-301 (DoD 5500.7-R.)).

5-2 Procedures

1. Managing Facsimile Services

    a. Limit transmissions requiring use of long distance services to time sensitive communications only.

    b. Send multiple documents that are going to the same location in batches rather than one at a time.

    c. Facsimile transmission cover sheets add to the cost of each transmission. Keep cover sheets as simple and functional as possible with only essential information. Avoid graphics and heavy gray or black areas because they slow transmissions and increase costs.

    (1) Instead of using separate cover sheets when sending material via facsimile transmission, commands are encouraged to procure a rubber stamp (1 inch by 4 inches) formatted as follows:

```
FROM:_____        TO:_____
ACTIVITY:_____      ACTIVITY_____
PHONE #:_____       PHONE #:_____
# OF PAGES:_____       # OF PAGES:_____

Replace thermal paper facsimiles that are records with photocopies.
```

    (2) Place the stamp at either the top, bottom, or side margin. This will eliminate the need for an extra page and save money, material, labor, energy, and time.

2. Security and Privacy Issues

    a. Do not transmit classified data via unsecured facsimile equipment. See SECNAV M-5510.36 and SECNAVINST 5211.5E, Department of the Navy Privacy Act (PA) Program, for more information regarding transmitting classified material via facsimile equipment.

    b. Follow established guidelines and exercise good judgment in transmitting sensitive information. See page 4-2, paragraph 4.

3.   Records Management

a.   Correspondence transmitted via a facsimile machine has the same authority as if it were the original. Normally the original is retained by the sending activity. The sender determines whether the correspondence is important enough to forward the original. If the original is forwarded, the advance copy becomes non-record material and may be destroyed by the receiving office once the original is received.

b.   Activities that receive many official documents via facsimile may need to procure a rubber stamp such as the one shown below to assist in identifying documents that are to be retained for record purposes.

ACTION COPY
DO NOT DESTROY

c.   Some facsimile machines still use thermal paper, which can deteriorate in as little as 6 months. Because of this, thermal paper facsimiles that need to be retained for record purposes should be photocopied.

CHAPTER 6
Postal Standards

6-1 **General**. This chapter includes U.S. Postal Service (USPS) standards and Navy policies pertaining to official mail. For additional information, refer to OPNAVINST 5218.7B, Navy Official Mail Management Instructions.

6-2 **Procedures**

1. Choosing the Right Size Envelope or Container. Use envelopes or mailing containers only slightly larger than the material being mailed and of sufficient strength to protect the contents during the mail handling process. Envelopes should be no smaller than 3 1/2 inches by 5 inches and no larger than 6 1/8 inches by 11 1/2 inches, if possible. Mail smaller than 3 1/2 inches by 5 inches cannot be mailed. You can send mail that is larger than 6 1/8 inches by 11 1/2 inches; however, it must bypass automated equipment and be processed through slower and less efficient methods. Reduce mailing expenses by following these steps:

    a. Use standard letter size (number 10) envelopes whenever possible. Generally, documents with four or less pages should be folded and mailed in a letter size envelope rather than a larger size envelope. See figure 6-1. The USPS automated processing equipment cannot handle envelopes thicker than 1/4 inch.

    b. Use large envelopes for material that cannot be folded (photographs, diplomas, negatives, and bulk material).

    c. Consolidate by class, all mail generated on the same day and destined for the same addressee.

    d. Check with your mailroom for activities/agencies within the local area that are serviced by couriers, as this requires no postage.

2. Sources of Address Information. Address official Navy mail to the command or activity addresses in:

    a. SNDL, parts 1 and 2.

    b. Https://www.manpower.usmc.mil/portal/page?_pageid=278,1&_dad=portal&_schema=PORTAL (Active Marine Link, Personal and Family Link, Military Personnel Services Link, Postal Link, under reference).

    c. Department of Defense Activity Address Directory (DoDAAD), DoD Manual 4000.25-6-M.

3. Delivery and Return Address Formats

   a. Requirements

      (1) Be sure you have the correct address and use organizational codes whenever possible.

      (2) Type, or print by other mechanical means, the delivery address in uppercase letters. Use no punctuation except for the hyphen in the ZIP+4 code. Use black or blue-black ribbon or ink. The return address may be preprinted, typewritten, or rubber stamped.

      (3) If available, use the ZIP+4 code and USPS acceptable abbreviations. Figure 6-2 is a listing of USPS acceptable abbreviations for streets and words that often appear in the names of places. A listing of acceptable USPS two-letter State and territory abbreviations appears in figure 6-3.

      (4) Do not use print styles that:

         (a) Incorporate proportional spacing,

         (b) have characters that overlap,

         (c) have highly styled characters such as script, italics, artistic, etc., or

         (d) have dots that do not touch to form each letter (dot matrix styles).

      (5) Limit official mail addresses (both delivery and return) to five lines. Format with a uniform left margin and a maximum of 47 characters per line, including spaces.

      (6) Center the address and single-space each line, blocked one below the other. Do not indent lines. Leave at least a 1-inch margin from the left and right edges of the envelope and at least 5/8 inch from the bottom of the envelope. The last line of the address should be no lower than 5/8 inch and no higher than 2 1/4 inches from the bottom of the envelope. Include all required information within addressee and return addressee areas. Do not type in the margins or clear area. Do not overlap the return address in the delivery address area. Be careful not to slant the address. The lines must be parallel to the top and bottom edges of the envelope. Refer to figure 6-4 for placement and format.

   b. Mail Sent Within the DoD. Prepare the address as follows:

      (1) Non-address Data Line - First Line (Optional). Use this to address official correspondence to the official in charge, such as commanding officer, director, commander, etc.

      (2) Information/Attention Line - Second Line (Optional). If known, place the name of the action officer, a specific individual, or section and code here.

(3) <u>Name of Recipient Line - Third Line</u>. Place the activity short title (less the city and state) here.

(4) <u>Delivery Address Line - Fourth Line</u>. Place either a street address or post office box number here. Use the word "SUITE" to designate locations within a building. See figure 6-2 for acceptable USPS street and places abbreviations.

(5) <u>Post Office Line - Fifth Line</u>. Place the city, state, and ZIP+4 code (in that order) here. Use the standard two-letter abbreviations shown in figure 6-3.

4. <u>Mail Classifications</u>. Select the class of mail service that meets the security, accountability, and delivery requirements of the material being shipped at the most economical cost. See OPNAVINST 5218.7B for the definitions of classes of mail and special supplemental postal services.

5. <u>Mail Markings</u>. Mark all mail, except first-class mail in a standard letter size (number 10) envelope, with the class of mail service you desire. Place the marking, i.e., first-class, priority, etc., in the upper right corner, about 1/4 inch below the postage meter imprint, mail stamp, or permit imprint. Mailings without a class of mail marking, except those in a number 10 envelope, will be assumed to contain no first-class material and will be sent as the lowest possible class of service.

Number 6-3/4 Envelopes (3 5/8" X 6 ½")

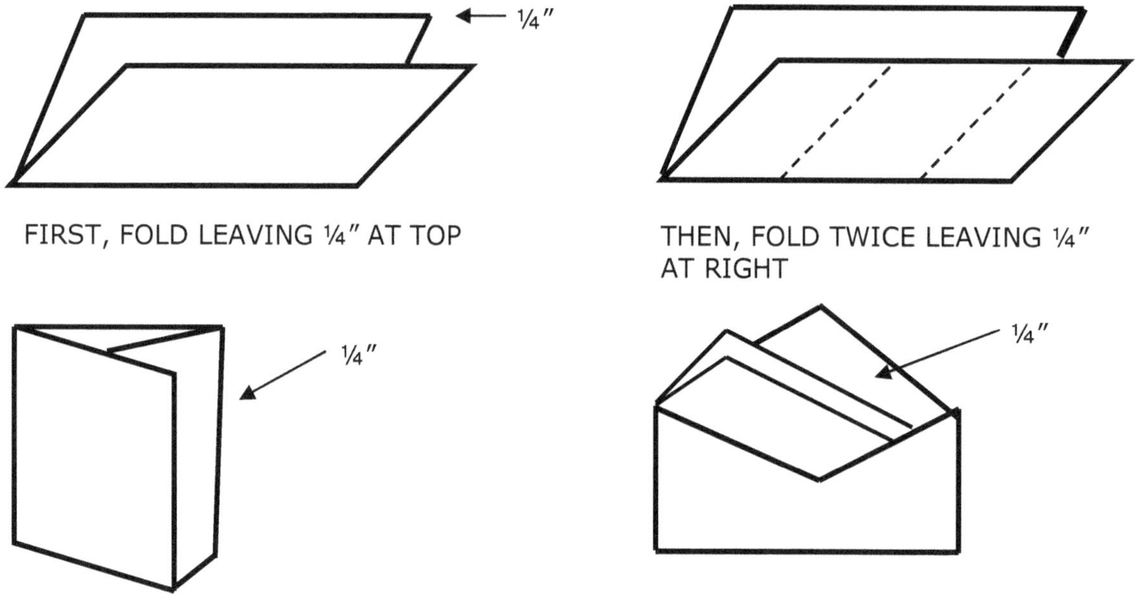

¼"

FIRST, FOLD LEAVING ¼" AT TOP

THEN, FOLD TWICE LEAVING ¼" AT RIGHT

¼"

¼"

Number 10 Envelope (4 1/8" X 9 ½")

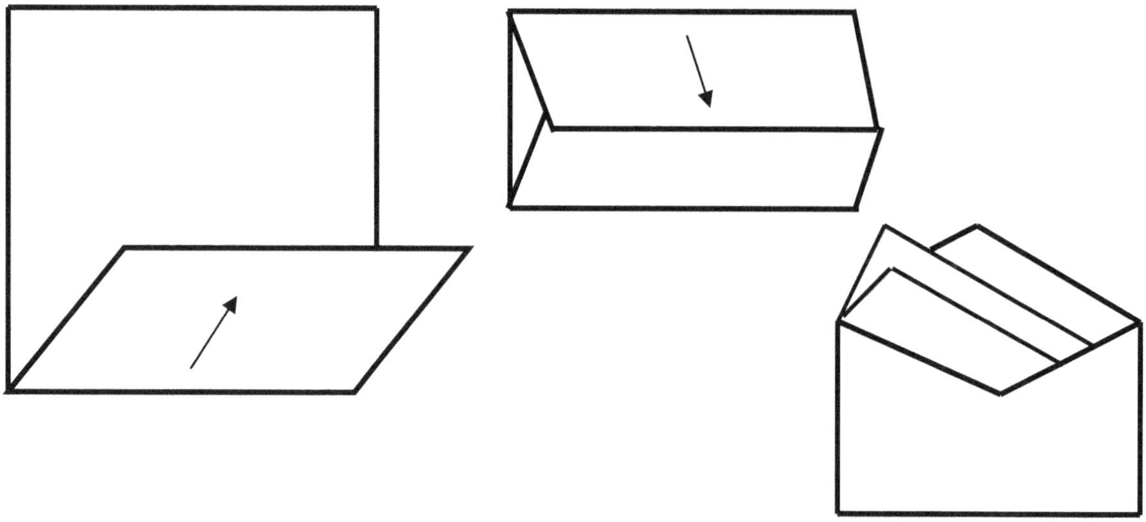

Window Envelope

FIGURE 6-1. FOLDING TECHNIQUES

Academy	ACAD	Fork	FRK	Place	PL
Agency	AGNCY	Fort	FT	Plain	PLN
Airport	ARPRT	Freeway	FWY	Plains	PLNS
Annex	ANX	Gardens	GDNS	Plaza	PLZ
Arcade	ARC	Gateway	GTWY	Point	PT
Avenue	AVE	Glen	GLN	Port	PRT
Bayou	BYU	Green	GRN	Prairie	PR
Beach	BCH	Grove	GRV	Radial	RADL
Bend	BND	Harbor	HBR	Ranch	RNCH
Bluff	BLF	Haven	HVN	Rapids	RPDS
Bottom	BTM	Heights	HTS	Rest	RST
Boulevard	BLVD	High	HI	Ridge	RDG
Branch	BR	Highway	HWY	River	RIV
Bridge	BRG	Hill	HL	Road	RD
Brook	BRK	Hills	HLS	Row	ROW
Burg	BG	Hollow	HOLW	Run	RUN
Bypass	BYP	Hospital	HOSP	Rural	R
Camp	CP	Inlet	INLT	Saint	ST
Canyon	CYN	Institute	INST	School	SCH
Cape	CPE	Island	IS	Shoal	SHL
Causeway	CSWY	Islands	ISS	Shoals	SHLS
Center	CTR	Isle	ISLE	Shore	SHR
Circle	CIR	Junction	JCT	Shores	SHRS
Cliffs	CLFS	Key	KY	South	S
Club	CLB	Knolls	KNLS	Spring	SPG
College	CLG	Lake	LK	Springs	SPGS
Corner	COR	Lakes	LKS	Spur	SPUR
Corners	CORS	Landing	LNDG	Square	SQ
Court	CT	Lane	LN	Station	STA
Courts	CTS	Light	LGT	Stravenue	STRA
Cove	CV	Loaf	LF	Stream	STRM
Creek	CRK	Locks	LCKS	Street	ST
Crescent	CRES	Lodge	LDG	Summit	SMT
Crossing	XING	Loop	LOOP	Terrace	TER
Dale	DL	Lower	LWR	Trace	TRCE
Dam	DM	Manor	MNR	Track	TRAK
Deport	DPO	Meadows	MDWS	Trail	TRL
Divide	DV	Mill	ML	Trailer	TRLR
Drive	DR	Mills	MLS	Tunnel	TUNL
East	E	Mission	MSN	Turnpike	TPKE
Estates	EST	Mount	MT	Union	UN
Expressway	EXPY	Mountain	MTN	University	UNIV
Extension	EXT	National	NAT	Valley	VLY
Fall	FALL	Neck	NCK	Viaduct	VIA
Falls	FLS	North	N	View	VW
Ferry	FRY	Orchard	ORCH	Village	VLG
Field	FLD	Oval	OVAL	Ville	VL
Fields	FLDS	Park	PARK	Vista	VIS
Flats	FLT	Parkway	PKY	Walk	WALK
Ford	FRD	Pass	PASS	Water	WTR
Forest	FRST	Path	PATH	Way	WAY
Forge	FRG	Pike	PIKE	Wells	WLS
Pillar	PLR	Pines	PNES	West	W

FIGURE 6-2. STANDARD ADDRESS ABBREVIATIONS

Alabama	AL		Montana	MT
Alaska	AK		Nebraska	NE
Arizona	AZ		Nevada	NV
Arkansas	AR		New Hampshire	NH
American Samoa	AS		New Jersey	NJ
California	CA		New Mexico	NM
Colorado	CO		New York	NY
Connecticut	CT		North Carolina	NC
Delaware	DE		North Dakota	ND
District of Columbia	DC		Northern Mariana Island	MP
Federated States of Micronesia	FM		Ohio	OH
Florida	FL		Oklahoma	OK
Georgia	GA		Oregon	OR
Guam	GU		Palau	PW
Hawaii	HI		Pennsylvania	PA
Idaho	ID		Puerto Rico	PR
Illinois	IL		Rhode Island	RI
Indiana	IN		South Carolina	SC
Iowa	IA		South Dakota	SD
Kansas	KS		Tennessee	TN
Kentucky	KY		Texas	TX
Louisiana	LA		Utah	UT
Maine	ME		Vermont	VT
Marshall Island	MH		Virginia	VA
Maryland	MD		Virgin Islands	VI
Massachusetts	MA		Washington	WA
Michigan	MI		West Virginia	WV
Minnesota	MN		Wisconsin	WI
Mississippi	MS		Wyoming	WY
Missouri	MO			

FIGURE 6-3. STATE/TERRITORY ABBREVIATIONS

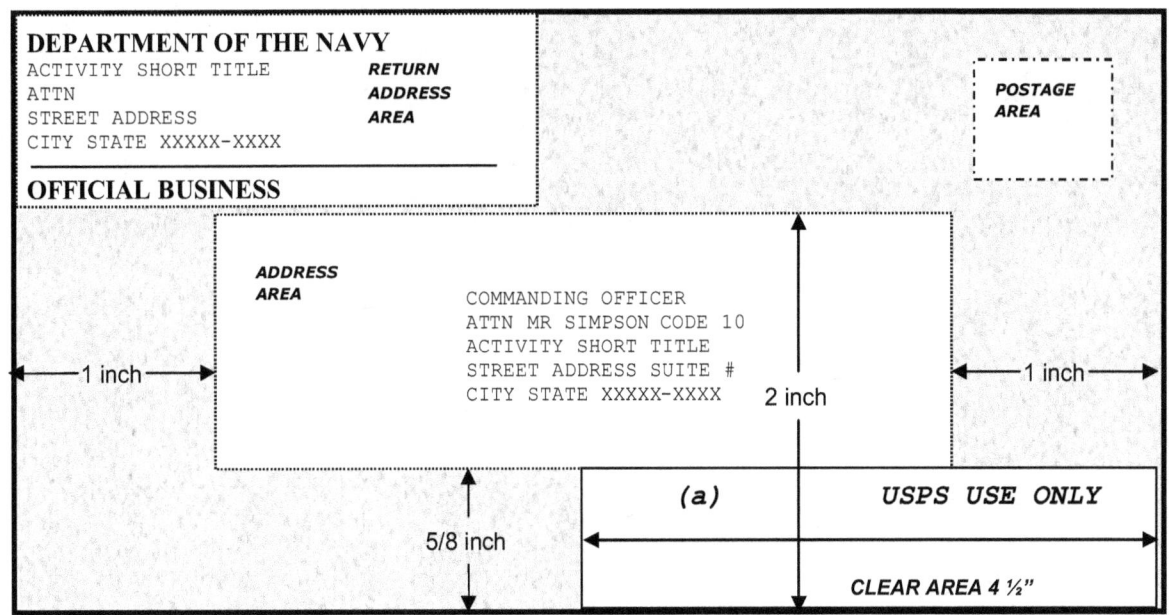

Ashore

COMMANDING OFFICER	(Title of Official in Charge)
ATTN LT JAY BREWER	(Action Officer, Organizational Code)
ACTIVITIY SHORT TITLE	(Activity Short Title (less City & State)
STREET ADDRESS SUITE #	(Street Address, Suite Number)
CITY STATE XXXXX-XXXX	(City State ZIP+4)

Afloat

COMMANDING OFFICER	(Title of Official in Charge)
ATTN ENS C D SUMMERHILL	(Action Officer, Organizational Code)
USS BLUESAIL DDG 00	(Name of Ship or Squadron)
FPO AP 12345-0876	(Fleet Post Office and its number)

Naval Personnel

AMAA JAMES E. SCENNA	(Addressee's Name)
VFX 1	(Name of Ship or Squadron)
FPO AP 12345-0876	(Fleet Post Office and its number)

Personal/Business/Bldg Name

ATTN MR STEVEN HOOD	(Personal Name)
AMERICAN AIRLINES CORP	(Business Name)
SKYSCRAPER BLDG 2	(Building Name and Number)
12345 S RUNWAY ST	(Street Address)
SKYLINE WA 54321-0123	(City State ZIP+4)

Standard Street Address

MR BERNARD G WATSON	(Addressee's Name)
112 45TH AVE E APT 3	(Street Address, Apartment Number)
SAVANNAH GA 23456-5431	(City State ZIP+4)

Foreign Addresses

MRS E BOATWRIGHT	(Addressee's Name)
101 INTERNATIONAL CIR	(Street Address)
LONDON WIPGHQ	(City, Postal Delivery Zone (If any)
ENGLAND	(County Name)

FIGURE 6-4. ENVELOPE ADDRESSING STANDARDS

THIS PAGE INTENTIONALLY LEFT BLANK

CHAPTER 7
Correspondence Formats

7-1 Requirements

1.   Use the standard letter format or one of its variations to correspond officially within or outside the DoD.

2.   The format of the standard letter, with slight variations, sets the pattern for joint letters, multiple-address letters, endorsements, directives, memoranda, etc. Refer to the two-page letter illustrations at figures 7-1 and 7-2. Figure 7-3 contains the formatting techniques to use when preparing a standard letter for use with a window envelope. Figure 7-4 is an example of a joint letter for joint release by two commands.

3.   The person whose title appears in the "To:" line is the action addressee. Aside from its one action addressee, the standard letter may have any number of "Via" addressees, "Copy to" addressees, or both. See chapter 8 to prepare a letter with more than one action addressee.

7-2 Format

1.   Margins. Allow 1-inch top, bottom, left, and right margins on each page. On letterhead paper, typing starts more than 1-inch from the top when the letterhead is printed. Do not right, center, or full justify text or use proportional spacing. For directives, headers are 1 inch and footers are .5 inches.

2.   Sender's Symbols. If "in reply refer to" is printed on your activity's letterhead paper, type the SSIC on the next line. If "in reply refer to" is not printed on your activity's letterhead paper, type the SSIC on the second line below the letterhead, starting 2 inches or more from the right edge of the paper. The longest line of the sender's symbol should end close to the right margin.

   a.   Authorized Sender's Symbols. A sender's symbol for a standard letter has three parts:

   (1)   Standard Subject Identification Code. An SSIC is a four- or five-digit number which represent a document's subject. They are used to categorize information by subject and are required on all Navy and Marine Corps letters or messages, directives, memos, forms, and reports. To find the SSIC that most closely represents the subject, refer to SECNAV M-5210.2,.

   (2)   Originator's Code, By Itself Or In a Serial Number. The originator's code, with or without the serial number, is the originator's office symbol or the hull number of a ship. Each command or activity will determine makeup of the originator's code.

   (a)   Originator's Code Without Serial Numbers. Start the originator's code immediately under the SSIC. Below are examples of two SSICs with only the originator's code:

```
EXAMPLE:      5216              5800
              Code 13          N00J
```

(b) <u>Originator's Code With Serial Numbers</u>. All classified correspondence created by your activity must be given a serial number. A serial number is not required on unclassified correspondence. Whether unclassified correspondence is serialized or not depends on local practice. Volume is the major criterion. An activity that produces little correspondence, and all of it is unclassified, probably does not need to use serial numbers. The added control must be weighed against the added complications of typing or stamping serial numbers. An activity that uses serial numbers shall start a new sequence of numbers at the beginning of each calendar year and assigns numbers consecutively beginning with 001.

(c) <u>Classified Markings</u>. Start the originator's code immediately under the SSIC followed by a forward slash with no spaces before or after the slash, the classification (if classified) (**C** for **Confidential**, S for Secret, T for Top Secret), and then the next unused serial number for the current calendar year. Below are two examples of a sender's symbol using the originator's code and serial number:

```
EXAMPLE:        5216                    5800
                Ser Code 13/271         Ser N00J/C20
```

(3) <u>Date</u>. Date a letter on the same day it is signed. Do not type the date when preparing correspondence that will be signed on a later date. Use the abbreviated date format discussed in chapter 2, page 2-11.

```
EXAMPLE:        5216                    5800
                Ser Code 13/271         Ser N00J/S20
                7 Sep 06                5 Jan 07
```

b. <u>Exceptions to Requirements for Using Identification Symbols</u>. Local practices determine how to use identification symbols in the following cases:

(1) Letters to members of Congress or heads of Government agencies.

(2) Letters of praise or condolence.

c. <u>Unauthorized Identification Symbols</u>. Numbers assigned by word processing centers and the initials of writers and typists are unauthorized as identification symbols; however, they may be included on file copies as part of the drafter's identification.

3. <u>Classified Correspondence</u>. You must have the right security clearance and know marking/handling requirements to prepare classified correspondence. An example of a classified letter is provided in figure 7-5. Refer to SECNAV M-5510.36 for additional information on marking and handling classified correspondence.

4. For Official Use Only

   a. For Official Use Only (FOUO) applies to information that is not classified, but which may be withheld from the public under the FOIA. Never use "For Official Use Only" as a classification to protect national security.

   b. To designate correspondence as FOUO, type "FOR OFFICIAL USE ONLY" in capital letters, centered at the bottom of the first and last page and any page that contains FOUO information. See figure 7-7. For documents with cover or title pages, type, stamp, or print in capital letters "FOR OFFICIAL USE ONLY" centered at the bottom on the front cover and the outside of the back cover. For additional information refer to SECNAV M-5510.36.

5. "From:" Line

   a. General. Every standard letter must have a "From:" line, except a letter that will be used with a window envelope. To prepare a letter for a window envelope, follow figure 7-3. As a general rule, the "From:" line is composed of the activity head's title and the activity's name. Refer to the three publications listed below for the correct names and mailing addresses for DON and DoD activities.

      (1) SNDL, Parts 1 and 2.

      (2) Https://www.manpower.usmc.mil/portal/page?_pageid=278,1&_dad=portal&_schema=PORTAL (Active Marine Link, Personal and Family Link, Military Personnel Services Link, Postal Link, under reference).

      (3) DoDAAD, DoD Manual 4000.25-6-M.

   b. Converting an SNDL Address to a "From:" Line Address. The "From:" line gives more than a title, but less than a full mailing address. Include enough information to distinguish your activity from other activities that may have the same name, but are in a different city or country. In some cases a one-of-kind title adequately identifies an activity and the location is unnecessary (e.g., "Secretary of the Navy"). The below examples show various way of converting SNDL addresses to "From:" line addresses.

```
EXAMPLE:

SNDL Entry                      From Line

COMMANDING OFFICER              Commanding Officer, Naval Station Norfolk
NAVAL STATION
NORFOLK VA 23511-6000

COMMANDING OFFICER              Commanding Officer, USS CHUNG-HOON (DDG 93)
USS CHUNG-HOON (DDG 93)
FPO AP 96662-1302
```

```
COMMANDING OFFICER          Commanding Officer, Patrol Squadron 45
VP 45
UNIT 60172
FPO AA 34099-5918
```

c. <u>Format</u>. Type "From:" at the left margin on the second line below the date line. The text begins two spaces after the colon. If the entry is longer than one line, start the second line under the first word after the heading.

```
EXAMPLE:

From: Commanding Officer, USS BLUE RIDGE (LCC 19)

From:  Commanding Officer, Naval Recruiting District Minneapolis,
       212 3rd Avenue South, Minneapolis, MN 55401-2592
```

d. <u>Avoid Multiple Titles</u>. If your commanding officer has more than one title, choose the title that corresponds with the content of the letter.

6. <u>"To:" Line</u>

a. <u>General</u>. Address all correspondence to the activity head of an activity. Include the office code or person's title that will act on your letter in parentheses, if known. If the office code is composed of only numbers, add the word "Code" before the numbers. Do not add the word "Code" before an office code that starts with a letter (e.g., "N" or "SUP"). Because frequent turnover in personnel can result in misrouted mail, avoid using the name of an individual in the "To:" line. You may use the complete mailing address and ZIP+4 code if you want the address for a record. If you will be using a window envelope, follow figure 7-3.

b. <u>Format</u>. Type "To:" at the left margin on the first line under the "From:" line (do not skip a line). Four spaces follow the colon.

```
EXAMPLE:

From:  Chief of Naval Operations
To:    Commanding Officer, USS JOHN C STENNIS (CVN 74)

From:  Assistant Secretary of the Navy (Financial Management and
       Comptroller)
To:    Chief of Naval Reserve

From:  Commanding Officer, Naval Station, San Diego (Code 10)
To:    Officer in Charge, Personnel Support Activity Detachment,
       China Lake, CA 93555-6001
```

7. "Via:" Line

    a. General. Use a "Via:" line when one or more activities outside of your activity should review a letter before it reaches the action addressee. The format for the "Via:" line is the same as for the "From:" line and "To:" line discussed in paragraphs 5 and 6 above.

    b. Format. Type "Via:" at the left margin on the first line below the "To:" line. Three spaces follow the colon. If the entry is longer than one line, start the second line under the first word after the heading.

```
EXAMPLE:

From:   Chief of Naval Operations
To:     Commander, U.S. Fleet Forces Command
Via:    Commander, U.S. Pacific Fleet
```

    c. Numbering Via Addressees. Number "Via" addressees if two or more are listed. Follow the chain of command. Routing starts with the addressee listed first.

```
EXAMPLE:

From:   Commander, Destroyer Squadron 23
To:     Commander, U.S. Fleet Forces Command
Via:    (1) Commander, Cruiser-Destroyer Group 1
        (2) Commander, Naval Surface Force, U.S. Pacific Fleet
        (3) Commander, U.S. Pacific Fleet
```

8. Subject Line

    a. General. The subject line consists of a sentence fragment that tells readers what the letter is about, usually in 10 words or less. Use normal word order and capitalize every letter after the colon. In formal correspondence, do not use acronyms in the subject line. If the subject appears elsewhere in the text of the letter, capitalize it using the "Title Case" format. When replying to a letter, repeat the subject of the incoming correspondence in the subject line, unless a change is essential for clarity.

    b. Format. Type "Subj:" at the left margin on the second line under the last line of the previous heading. Two spaces follow the colon. If the entry is longer than one line, line the second line under the first word after the heading.

```
EXAMPLE:

Subj:   PROGRAM ACQUISITION PROCESS FOR THE ADVANCED SEA-BASED
        TARGET PROFILING RADAR
```

9. Reference Line

a. General. Use only those references that bear directly on the subject at hand. Avoid unnecessary or complicated references. Many letters may not need a reference, while others are complete with a reference to only the latest communication in a series. List references in the order they appear in the text. Always mention cited references in the text. Additionally, when citing a reference it is not necessary to include the subject of the reference. However, the subject may be included, following all other required elements, if it aids in clarifying or better identifying the reference.

b. Avoiding Most NOTAL References. A not-to-all (NOTAL) reference is a document that some addressees neither hold nor need. Avoid NOTAL references whenever possible. If a NOTAL reference is unavoidable, follow the reference in the reference line with the term "NOTAL" in parentheses. The following paragraphs discuss various referencing situations and an appropriate action for each situation:

(1) If it is known that the action addressee does not have a reference listed in your correspondence, include it as an enclosure to your correspondence or refer to it in the text. Enclosing an existing document as an enclosure is not allowed in directives.

EXAMPLE: (Referencing a NOTAL reference in the text of the correspondence.)

"CNO WASHINGTON DC 121845Z Mar 07 directed all afloat Navy activities to provide statistical data on fuel usage. Request you provide the requested data by 1 June 2007."

(2) If you would like to provide a copy of a reference listed in your correspondence to a "Via" or "Copy to" addressee, annotate "w/ref (x)" in parentheses to the right of the addressee you send it to. (Substitute the appropriate reference letter for x.) Only include this annotation on the copy for the addressee you are sending the reference to. Do not include the distribution of a reference to "Via" or "Copy to" addressees on the original letter.

EXAMPLE:

```
From:  Chief of Naval Operations
To:    Commander, U.S. Fleet Forces Command
Via:   Commander, U.S. Pacific Fleet (w/ref (c))

Copy to:
COMNAVPERSCOM (w/ref (a))
```

c. Format. Type "Ref:" at the left margin on the second line below the subject line. Use a lowercase letter in parentheses before the description of every reference. If you have only one reference, list it as "Ref: (a)". Three spaces follow the colon. References are listed in alphabetical order, a through z. If you have more than 26 references, continue with (aa), (ab), etc. If the entry is longer than one line, line the second line under the first word after the heading.

EXAMPLE:

Ref: (a) COMSUBGRU TWO ltr 7200 Ser N1/123 of 12 Mar 08

Ref: (ab) SECNAV M-5510.36

d. Citing Various Types of References

(1) Naval correspondence requires (a) the SNDL originator short title, (b) the type of correspondence ("ltr" or "memo"), (c) the SSIC, (d) the originator's code by itself or in a serial number, and (e) the date. If the reference was not dated, type "(undated)" as illustrated below.

EXAMPLE:

USS SEAWOLF ltr 7200 Ser SSN 21/124 of 19 Apr 07
USS PORTER ltr 5216 Ser DDG 78/437 of 7 Mar 06 (NOTAL)
CNO memo 5216 Ser 09B33/6U317731 (undated)

(2) A business letter requires (a) the company name, (b) the term "ltr", and (c) the date.

EXAMPLE:

Smith Widget Co. ltr of 14 Oct 05

(3) An e-mail requires (a) the SNDL originator's short title, (b) the term "e-mail," (c) the type of correspondence ("ltr" or "memo"), (d) the SSIC, (e) the originator's code by itself or in a serial number, and (f) the date.

EXAMPLE:

OPNAV e-mail ltr 5216 Ser N4/158 of 21 Sep 06

(4) A message requires (a) the originator's Plain Language Address as shown in the "From:" line of the message (if listed, do not include the office code) and (b) the complete date-time-group. When referencing general messages, include in parentheses the general message type (All Navy (ALNAV), Naval Administrative (NAVADMIN), All Marine Corps (ALMAR), etc.) and number/year.

EXAMPLE:

USS PORTER 071300Z Mar 04
NAS NORFOLK VA 101300Z Mar 06
CNO WASHINGTON DC 111300Z Mar 07 (NAVADMIN 123/09)

(5) Endorsements cite references depending on whether you want to mention them in passing or highlight a particular one.

EXAMPLE:

ENS Joe J. Mainville, USNR, XXX-XX-6789/1105 ltr of 1 Apr 97 w/ends

CONNAVSURFPAC THIRD ENDORSEMENT 1070 Ser N1/3124 of 22 Apr 97 to ENS Joe J. Mainville, USNR, XXX-XX-6789/1105 ltr of 1 Apr 97

(6) A telephone conversation or meeting requires (a) "PHONCON" or "Mtg"; (b) the activity's SNDL short title, the office code, the individual's name, and (c) the date. Follow the information for the first individual with a forward slash and repeat the information for the second individual.

EXAMPLES:

PHONCON CNO (N09B2) Ms. Handy/COMNAVAIRLANT (N6) CDR Phillips of 17 Feb 09

Mtg COMSUBGRU TWO (N1) YNCS(SS) Foster/SECNAV YNCS(SW/AW) Simpson of 9 Dec 09

(7) A Navy instruction requires (a) the SNDL short title combined with the term "INST" and (b) the SSIC with the consecutive number and, if any, a revision letter. If referencing a large instruction, do not call out the chapter, section, or paragraph in the reference line, instead, identify them when using the reference in the text of the correspondence.

EXAMPLES:

NAVSUPINST 7510.1
SECNAV M-5216.5, Department of the Navy (DON) Correspondence Manual

(identifying an enclosure, chapter, section or paragraph of a reference in the text)
"Reference (a), enclosure (3), paragraph 11a(2) requires …"

(8) A Navy notice requires (a) the SNDL short title of issuer combined with the term "NOTE" and the SSIC, (b) the serial number, (c) the date, and (d) the cancellation date enclosed in parenthesis (e.g., (Canc: Aug 08)). If referencing a large notice, do not call out the chapter, section, or paragraph in the reference line, instead, identify them when using the reference in the text of the correspondence.

EXAMPLE:

OPNAVNOTE 5216 Ser 09B/6U709210 of 21 May 08 (Canc: May 09)

(9) A DoD directive or instruction requires (a) the short title of issuer with either Instruction or Directive, (b) the SSIC with consecutive number, and (c) the date with the month spelled out. If referencing a large instruction or directive, do not call out the chapter, section, or paragraph in the reference line, instead, identify them when using the reference in the text of the correspondence.

```
EXAMPLE:

DoD Directive 2000.1 of 6 May 2006
DoD Instruction 1995.1 of 4 April 2008
```

(10) A DoD publication requires (a) the short title of issuer (b) the publication number, (c) the publication type, (d) the title, and (e) the date.

```
EXAMPLE:

DoDD 4000.25-R-1, DoD Logistics Data Element Dictionary/
Directory, January 1990
DoD 5200.28-M, ADP Security Manual (C3I), January 1973
```

(11) A form requires (a) the issuer, (b) the form number, and (c) the issue or revision date.

```
EXAMPLE:

NAVJAG 5800/15 (Rev. 7-1996)
```

(12) A report that has a Report Control Symbol requires (a) the report title, (b) the issuer, and (c) the report number.

```
EXAMPLE:

Injury Report (NAVJAG 5800-19)
```

(13) A Navy publication requires (a) the issuer and (b) the publication number.

```
EXAMPLE:

NAVPERS 15018
```

(14) Code of Federal Regulations requires (a) the title number, (b) the term "CFR", (c) the part or chapter number, and (d) the section number (optional).

```
EXAMPLE:

41 CFR 201-45.000
```

(15) Federal Register (FR) requires (a) the volume number, (b) the term "FR", and (c) the page number.

EXAMPLE:

21 FR 623

(16) A United States Code requires (a) the title number, (b) the term "U.S.C.", (c) the section symbol (§), and (d) the section number. Do not include spaces in the term "U.S.C."

EXAMPLE:

28 U.S.C. §1498

(17) An Executive Order requires (a) the term "E.O." and (b) the order number.

EXAMPLE:

E.O. 12564

(18) "My" and "Your" Optional. To cite an earlier communication between your activity and the action addressee, you may substitute a personal pronoun for the issuing activity. To prevent confusion, avoid "my" and "your" in the reference line of a letter that has more than one action addressee.

EXAMPLES:

My ltr 5216 Ser Code 10/049 of 2 Sep 09
Your msg 221501Z Aug 09

10. Enclosure Line

    a.   General. List enclosures in the enclosure line in the order they appear in the text. Identify an enclosure using the same format as you would when identifying a reference. See paragraph 9 above. When identifying a document, cite its subject or title exactly. Never list an item in both the enclosure line and reference line of the same letter.

    b.   Format. Type "Encl:" at the left margin on the second line below the last line of the previous heading. Two spaces follow the colon. Use a number in parentheses before the description of every enclosure, even if you have only one. One space follows the closing parenthesis. If the entry is longer than one line, start the second line under the first word after the heading.

```
EXAMPLE:

Encl:   (1) List of Reserve Officers Selected for Promotion to
            Colonel
        (2) CMC ltr 5216 Ser 00/451 of 5 Sep 09
        (3) SECNAVINST 1400.1
```

c. <u>Normal Distribution and When to Vary It</u>. Normally, send one copy of the basic letter plus any enclosures to all addressees. Do not use the term "w/encl" to indicate that all addressees are being sent the enclosures. Avoid sending an enclosure if an addressee has it already or if its bulk or other factors make furnishing it impractical.

d. <u>Adding Copies of Enclosures for all Addressees</u>. When sending more than one copy of an enclosure to all addressees ("To," "Via," and "Copy to"), note the quantity in parentheses after the enclosure's description.

```
EXAMPLE:

Encl:   (1) OPNAV 5216/10 (10 Copies)
```

e. <u>Variations Affecting Only Copy To Addressees</u>. In certain circumstances, it may be necessary to vary the normal distribution of enclosures to "Copy to" addressees. It is up to the originator of the correspondence to make this determination. There are two basic methods of varying distribution; all "Copy to" addressees are affected or only one or a few of the "Copy to" addressees are affected.

(1) In these examples, all "Copy to" addressees are affected in the same way, so notes appear beside the "Copy to" heading.

```
EXAMPLE:

Copy to:   (w/o encls)
Copy to:   (w/o encls (2) and (3))
Copy to:   (w/2 copies of encl (1))
```

(2) In this example, only some of the "Copy to" addressees are affected, so notes appear beside the affected addressees.

```
EXAMPLE:

Copy to:
COMNAVSURFPAC (N1) (w/o encls)
USS MUSTIN (w/encl (2) only)
USS VANDERGRIFT
```

f. <u>Variations Affecting Only Via Addressees</u>. When varying the normal distribution of enclosures to "Via" addressees, show the variation beside the affected addressee. One possible variation appears below. Others may be adapted for the examples in paragraph 10e above.

```
EXAMPLE:

Via:    Commanding Officer, Naval Technical Training Center,
        Meridian (w/o encl)
```

g. <u>Sending Enclosures Separately</u>. When size, weight, or other factors prevent sending an enclosure with a letter, send it separately and type the term "sep cover" in parentheses after the enclosure's description.

```
EXAMPLE:

Encl:   (1) SECNAV M-5216.5 (sep cover)
```

11. <u>Text</u>. Start the text on the second line down from the previous entry. The text shall be left justified. Make the content clear by using plain English. Do not use slang or jargon. Refer to chapter 12 for guidance on writing.

12. <u>Paragraphs</u>. Start all continuation lines at the left margin. All paragraphs are single spaced and each paragraph or subparagraph begins on the second line below the previous paragraph or subparagraph. When using a subparagraph, the first line is always indented the appropriate number of spaces depending on the level of subparagraphing. All other lines of a subparagraph continue at the left margin. Do not indent the continuation lines of a subparagraph. If there is a paragraph 1a, there must be a paragraph 1b; if there is a paragraph 1a(1), there must be a paragraph 1a(2), etc. It is acceptable for a paragraph to break across pages, but do not begin a paragraph at the bottom of a page unless there is enough space for at least two lines of text on that page and at least two lines of text are carried over to the next page. A signature page must have at least two lines of text preceding the signature.

a. <u>Identifying Paragraphs or Subparagraphs</u>. Identify all paragraphs or subparagraphs with a number or letter. See figure 7-8 for an example of paragraph and subparagraph structure and identification.

b. <u>Limit Subparagraphs</u>. Documents rarely require subdividing to the extent shown in figure 7-8. <u>Do not subdivide past the second level</u> until you have exhausted all re-paragraphing alternatives first. Never subparagraph beyond the levels shown in figure 7-8.

c. <u>Citing Paragraphs</u>. When citing a paragraph or subparagraph, write the numbers and letters without periods or spaces.

```
Example:   2b(4)(a)
```

d. <u>Paragraph Headings</u>. Use paragraph headings in long correspondence with widely varying topics. Be brief but informative. Underline any heading and capitalize its key words using the Title Case format. Be consistent across main paragraphs and subparagraphs. If paragraph 1 has a heading, then paragraph 2 would need a heading; if paragraph 1a has a heading, then paragraph 1b would need a heading.

13. Signature Line

a. General

(1) Only the original, which goes to the action addressee, must be signed; however, the original and all copies must have typed or stamped signature line information below the signature. The last name appears in all capital letters with the exception of a last name beginning with a prefix.

EXAMPLE: (last name beginning with a prefix)

                                          J. A. McBREARTY

(2) Start all lines of the signature line at the center of the page, beginning on the fourth line below the text. The preferred way to identify the signatory is by typing their first initial, middle initial, and last name. If the signatory does not have a middle name, use only their first initial and last name. Signature lines can be changed based on the signers preference. Do not include the signatory's rank or a complimentary close. Add the signature line only when you are sure who will sign the correspondence. If you use a stamp, remember to mark all copies and avoid smeared or crooked impressions. Refer to chapter 2, page 2-4 for delegation of signature authority guidance.

b. Examples of Signature Lines

(1) When an activity head will sign the correspondence, the signature line is composed of only their name.

EXAMPLE:
                                          C. R. FIRMAN

(2) When a principal subordinate authorized to sign by title, such as the chief of staff or deputy in a major command will sign the correspondence, include their title as the second line of the signature line.

EXAMPLE:
                                          R. O. DAVIDSON, III
                                          Deputy

(3) When an individual has been formally appointed to temporarily replace the commanding officer or a subordinate who signs by title, include the term "Acting" as the last line of the signature line.

EXAMPLES:

```
              C. ESCOBAR          H. T. MAC
              Acting              Deputy
                                  Acting
```

(4) Put the term "By direction" under the name of a subordinate formally authorized to sign official correspondence, but not by their title.

EXAMPLE:

```
                            L. AVALOS
                            By direction
```

(5) When the signatory is authorized to sign "by direction," and the correspondence will affect pay and allowances, the signature line will include the signatory's (a) name, (b) title, and (c) the phrase, "By direction of the [activity head]." (Insert the appropriate activity head title).

EXAMPLE:

```
                            E. ESPINOSA
                            Executive Officer
                            By direction of the
                            Commanding Officer
```

14. "Copy To:" Line

a. General. Use this optional line to list addressees outside your activity who need to know a letter's content but do not need to act on it. If you use the "Copy to:" line, keep the number of activities to a minimum.

b. Format. Type "Copy to:" at the left margin on the second line below the signature line. Identify addressees by their SNDL short title and/or SNDL numbers shown there. The SNDL number is an alpha-numeric number that is used to group commands or activities by classification. Do not list offices within the same activity individually, group them together in parentheses after the entry.

c. Variations. "Copy to" addressees are normally listed in a single column at the left margin and single spaced below the "Copy to:" line. A long list of copy to addressees can be listed in columns, as a paragraph, or may be continued on the next page or placed entirely on a new page. If the signature line of the correspondence is at the bottom of the page and the "Copy to:" line will not fit on that page, type "Copy to: (see next page)" to indicate that the "Copy to:" line is on the next page. Use this format for the "Distribution:" lines as well.

EXAMPLE: (Grouping of offices of an activity)

```
Copy to:
CNO (N1, N2, N3/5)
```

```
BUPERS (PERS 313C, PERS 49)
USS YORKTOWN (CG 48) (Code 01)


EXAMPLE:   (Large list in column format)


Copy to:
CNO (N1, N2, N3/5)              USS YORKTOWN (CG 48) (ADMIN)
BUPERS (PERS 313C)             USS MUSTIN (DDG 89)
COMCARSTRKGRU ELEVEN           USS BLUE RIDGE (LCC 19)


EXAMPLE:   (Large list in paragraph format)


Copy to:
CNO (N1, N2, N3/5), BUPERS (PERS 313C), COMCARSTRKGRU ELEVEN,
USS YORKTOWN (CG 48) (ADMIN), USS MUSTIN (DDG 89)


EXAMPLE:   (Continuation to a second page)


Copy to:  (Cont'd)
COMCARSTRKGRU ELEVEN
USS YORKTOWN (CG 48) (ADMIN)
USS MUSTIN (DDG 89)
```

15. <u>Identifying Second and Later Pages</u>. Repeat the subject line at the top of each page of the basic letter. Start typing at the left margin on the sixth line from the top of the page. Continue the text beginning on the second line below the subject.

16. <u>Page Numbering</u>. Do not number a single-page letter or the first page of a multiple-page letter. Center page numbers 1/2 inch from the bottom edge, starting with the number 2. No punctuation accompanies a page number. See figure 7-2. To number the pages of a TOP SECRET document, see SECNAV M-5510.36.

17. <u>Correspondence Package Assembly</u>. The basic letter, the enclosures, and the background material are assembled according to activity practices before they are presented for approval and signature. Figure 7-9 illustrates an assembled correspondence package that is ready for signature and mailing.

18. <u>Tabbing a Correspondence Package</u>. Tab the signature page (if not the first page), enclosures, and background material. Label the tabs as appropriate. Figure 7-10 illustrates an assembled correspondence package with tabs. Take care so tabs can be removed without defacing the document.

DEPARTMENT OF THE NAVY
NAME OF ACTIVITY
ADDRESS
CITY STATE ZIP+4

```
                                    SSIC
                                    Code/Serial #
                                    Date
    %
From:**Activity head, name of activity, location when
*******needed
To:****Title, name of activity (Code), location when
*******needed
Via:***(1)*Title, name of activity (Code), location
***********when needed
*******(2)*Same as Via (1) above
%
Subj:**NORMAL WORD ORDER WITH ALL LETTERS CAPITALIZED
*******AND NO PUNCTUATION
%
Ref:***(a)*Communication or document that bears
***********directly on the subject at hand
%
Encl:**(1)*Title of Material - enclosed with letter
*******(2)*Title of Material (sep cover) - not
************enclosed with letter
%
1.**This example shows the first page of a two-page
standard letter.  Included are many of the elements that
might appear on a standard letter.
%
2.**Start the "From:" line on the second line below the
date line.  The date may be typed or stamped.
%
3.**Arrange paragraphs as shown in figure 7-8.
%
****a.**Do not start a paragraph at the bottom of the page
unless at least two lines of text will remain on that page
and at least two lines of text will carry over to the next
page.
%
****b.**Do not number the first page, number only
succeeding pages.
```

```
┌─────────────────────┐
│ *  - Space          │
│ %  - Hard Return    │
└─────────────────────┘
```

FIGURE 7-1. STANDARD LETTER – FIRST PAGE

```
Subj:**REPEAT THE SUBJECT EXACTLY AS IT IS WRITTEN ON
*******THE FIRST PAGE OF THE LETTER
%
****c.**The second and succeeding pages of a standard
letter look like this:
%
********(1)*Start typing on the sixth line (1-inch top
margin).  Repeat the subject line.
%
********(2)*Continue the text on the second line below the
subject line.
%
4.**"Copy to" addressees appear on all copies.  "Blind
copy to" addressees, as well as the identity of the writer
and typist, appear on internal copies only.

5.**A standard letter uses no complimentary close.
%
%
%
                              NAME OF SIGNER
                              By direction
%
Copy to:
SNDL number and/or short title of information addressee
SNDL number and/or short title of 2nd information addressee
%
Blind copy to:
List blind copy addressees
```

```
* - Space
% - Hard Return
```

2

FIGURE 7-2. STANDARD LETTER – SECOND PAGE

DEPARTMENT OF THE NAVY
NAVY PERSONNEL COMMAND
5720 INTEGRITY DRIVE
MILLINGTON TN 38055-0130

5216
Ser 301/403
5 Oct 06

%
COMMANDER
NAVY PERSONNEL COMMAND (PERS-40)
5720 INTEGRITY DRIVE
MILLINGTON TN 38055-0130
%
%
%
%
Subj:**WINDOW-ENVELOPE FORMAT
%
1.**You may use a GSA general-purpose window envelope
(overall size 9-1/2 by 4-1/8 inches and window, 4-3/4 by 1-
1/4 inches, in lower left) if:
%
****a.**The address has no more than five lines, and does
not extend past the middle of the page. The complete
address must appear in the window with at least a 1/8-inch
margin, even if the letter shifts in the envelope.
%
****b.**The letter and enclosures are all unclassified.
%
****c.**Your letter does not have any "Via" addresses.
%
2.**Because this letter does not have a "From:" line, every
copy that goes to addressees outside your activity must be
on letterhead to show its origin.
%
3.**To fold the letter first turn up the bottom edge so it
just covers the subject, second, turn back the address
portion so the upper fold also falls along the top of the
subject.
%
%
%

A. J. ANGLIN
By direction

```
* - Space
% - Hard Return
```

FIGURE 7-3. STANDARD LETTER – WINDOW – ENVELOPE

DEPARTMENT OF THE NAVY
NAVAL SEA SYSTEMS COMMAND (20362-5101)
NAVAL SUPPLY SYSTEMS COMMAND (20376-5000)
WASHINGTON, DC

```
NAVSUP                                    NAVSEA
5216                                      5216
Ser 02/318                                Ser 07/207
9 Apr 06                                  17 Apr 06
%
JOINT LETTER
%
From:**Commander, Naval Sea Systems Command
******Commander, Naval Supply Systems Command
%
To:****Chief of Naval Operations
%
Subj:**HOW TO PREPARE A JOINT LETTER
%
1.**A joint letter may be used to establish an agreement
between two or more activities or for other matters of mutual
concern.  To prepare a Joint Memorandum, replace JOINT LETTER
with JOINT MEMORANDUM above the "From:" line.
%
2.**On plain bond paper, list the command titles in the
letterhead so the senior is at the top.  If the activities are
in different cities or states, follow each title with its
Standard Navy Distribution List address.
%
3.**Arrange signature lines so the senior official is at the
right.  Place the signature line of a third cosigner in the
middle of the page.  The senior official signs the letter
last.
%
4.**If your activity is the last to sign, send copies of the
signed letter to all cosigners.
%
%
%
J. J. SMITH                      M. L. JONES
Acting                           Deputy
```

| * - Space |
| % - Hard Return |

FIGURE 7-4. JOINT LETTER

SECRET

DEPARTMENT OF THE NAVY
OFFICE OF THE CHIEF OF NAVAL OPERATIONS
2000 NAVY PENTAGON
WASHINGTON DC 20350-2000

```
                                        5216
                                        Ser N09N/S391
                                        11 May 06
%
From:**Vice Chief of Naval Operations
To:****Commander, U.S. Pacific Command
%
Subj:**CLASSIFICATION MARKINGS (U)
%
1.**(U)*This is an example of a classified letter.  Each
paragraph shall be predicated with a portion marking.
%
****a.**(S)* Identify the classification of each paragraph.
This subparagraph is marked as SECRET as indicated by the (S)
portion marking.
%
****b.**(C)* Classification markings eliminate doubt as to
which portions of a document contain or reveal classified
information
%
2.**(U)*Stamp the letter's highest classification in the center
of the top and bottom margins.  Assign a serial number bearing
the initial of the highest classification.
%
3.**(U)*On the first page of a letter that contains classified
material, include associated markings.  The example below is
for a derivatively classified document.
%
4.**(U)*There are numerous rules and requirements for properly
marking classified correspondence.  This figure is a basic
example.  Figure 2-6 briefly discusses how to correctly mark an
unclassified letter of transmittal that has classified
enclosures.  Refer to SECNAV M-5510.36, chapter 6 for a
detailed description of how to properly mark classified
correspondence.
%
Derived from:**Multiple Sources
Declassify on:*10 Jun 15
```

```
* - Space
% - Hard Return
```

SECRET

{Classified for illustration purposes only}

FIGURE 7-5. STANDARD LETTER WITH CLASSIFICATION MARKINGS - FIRST PAGE

SECRET

Subj:**CLASSIFICATION MARKINGS (U)
%
5.**(U)*When typing an <u>unclassified letter that has a</u> <u>classified enclosure</u>, only these three steps are necessary.
%
****a.**(U) Type a classification statement on the second line below the date line.
%
EXAMPLE:

SECRET—Unclassified upon removal of enclosure (1)
%
****b.**(U) Indicate that the subject or title of the enclosure is unclassified.
%
EXAMPLE:

Encl: (1) Sample Classified Enclosure (U)
%
****c.**(U) Stamp the enclosure's classification in the center of the top and bottom margins of the letter of transmittal.
%
%
%

                              J. K. ELL
                              By direction

SECRET

2

* - Space	
% - Hard Return	

{Classified for illustration purposes only}

FIGURE 7-6. STANDARD LETTER WITH CLASSIFICATION MARKINGS-SECOND PAGE

DEPARTMENT OF THE NAVY
NAVY PERSONNEL COMMAND
5720 INTEGRITY DRIVE
MILLINGTON TN 38055-0130

```
                                        5216
                                        Ser N09L/729
                                        25 Jun 98
%
From:**Commander, Navy Personnel Command
To:****Commander in Chief, U.S. Naval Forces, Europe
%
Subj:**FOR OFFICIAL USE ONLY MARKINGS (FOUO)
%
1.**(FOUO) This illustrates a letter that has "For Official
Use Only" (FOUO) information.  Mark the bottom front cover
(if any), interior pages of documents, and on the outside
back cover (if any) with "FOR OFFICIAL USE ONLY".
%
2.**(FOUO) Subjects, titles and each section part,
paragraph, and similar portion of an FOUO document requiring
protection shall be portion marked.  Place the abbreviation
"(FOUO)" immediately following the portion letter or number,
or in the absence of letters or numbers, immediately before
the beginning of the portion.  Unclassified letters of
transmittal with FOUO enclosures or attachments shall be
marked at the top left corner with "FOR OFFICIAL USE ONLY
ATTACHMENT".
%
3.**For more information on designating and marking material
FOUO, refer to SECNAV M-5510.36.
%
%
%

                             R. D. DAVIDSON
                             By direction
```

```
+---------------------+
| *  -  Space         |
| %  -  Hard Return   |
+---------------------+
```

{Marking for illustration purposes only}

FOR OFFICIAL USE ONLY

FIGURE 7-7. STANDARD LETTER WITH FOUO MARKINGS

```
1.**Arrange paragraphs following the formats below.  See
chapter 2, page 7-11 for additional guidelines.
%
2.**If subparagraphs are needed, use at least two; e.g., a
(1) must have a (2).
%
****a.**Indent each new subdivision four spaces and start
typing at the fifth space.
%
****b.**Text
%
*******(1)*Documents rarely require subdividing to the
extent shown below.
%
*******(2)*Text
%
***********(a)*Do not subparagraph past this level until
you have exhausted all re-paragraphing alternatives.
%
***********(b)*Text
%
***************1.**Text
%
*******************a.**Text
%
***********************(1)*Text
%
***************************(a)*Never subparagraph beyond
this level.
%
***************************(b)*Text
%
***********************(2)*Text
%
*******************b.**Text
%
***************2.**Text
```

```
10.**When using two digits, continue to indent each new
subdivision four spaces and start typing on the fifth space
(paragraphs will not line up).
%
****a.**Text
%
*******(9)*Text
%
*******(10)*Text
```

*	– Space
%	– Hard Return

FIGURE 7-8. PARAGRAPH STRUCTURE FORMAT

Here is a suggested way to assemble a standard letter for signature and mailing. If you use a folder rather than the single stack of papers shown, clip items 1 and 9 to the left side and 2 through 8 to the right side of the folder.

Tab signature page, enclosures, and background material.

Check or arrow the intended addressee on each copy.

Prepare envelopes or mailing labels according to local practice. Your activity might not require them for addressees listed in the SNDL.

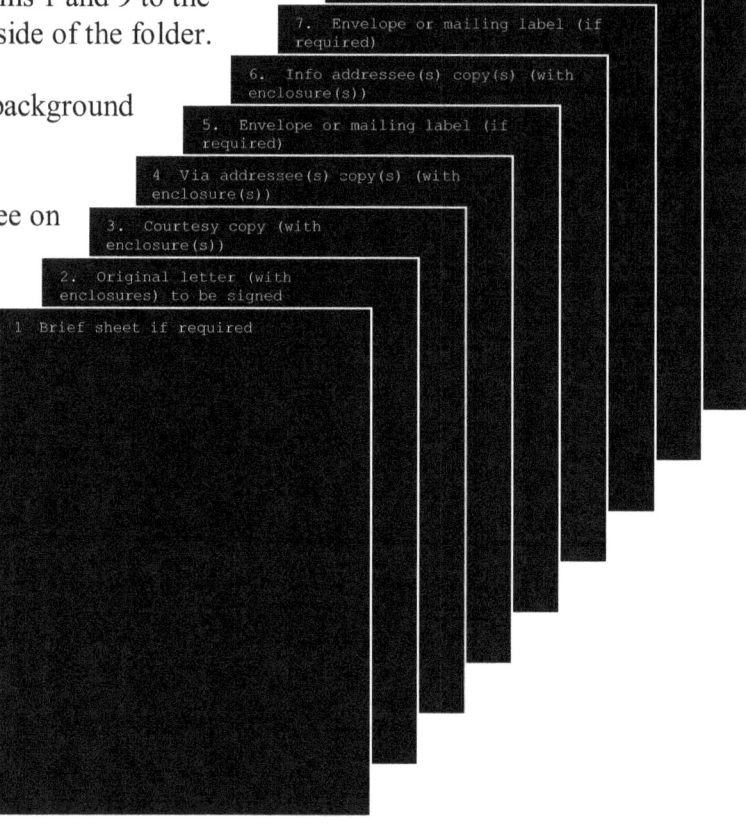

9. Background material

8. Official file copy (with enclosure(s))

7. Envelope or mailing label (if required)

6. Info addressee(s) copy(s) (with enclosure(s))

5. Envelope or mailing label (if required)

4. Via addressee(s) copy(s) (with enclosure(s))

3. Courtesy copy (with enclosure(s))

2. Original letter (with enclosures) to be signed

1. Brief sheet if required

BEFORE SIGNATURE

1. Briefing sheet as prescribed locally, usually omitted if letter is short or self-explanatory.
2. Original letter to be signed (signature tabbed if not on first page), pages in normal order, with enclosures.
3. Courtesy copy with enclosures, rarely used except with responses to congressional inquiries.
4. Copies for via addressees, if any, each with enclosures.
5. Envelope or mailing label, if required.
6. Copies for "Copy to:" addressees, each with enclosures.
7. Envelope or mailing label, if required.
8. Official file copy of letter with enclosures. Expose the left margin so reviewers can initial and date there.
9. Background material.

AFTER SIGNATURE

File

Mail

File

FIGURE 7-9. ASSEMBLY OF A STANDARD CORRESPONDENCE PACKAGE USING STACKING METHOD

The example on the right illustrates tabbing correspondence packages when correspondence is in the natural order using the stacking method.

Tab 1 - Signature Tab
Tab 2 - Enclosure Tabs
Tab 3 - Background Material

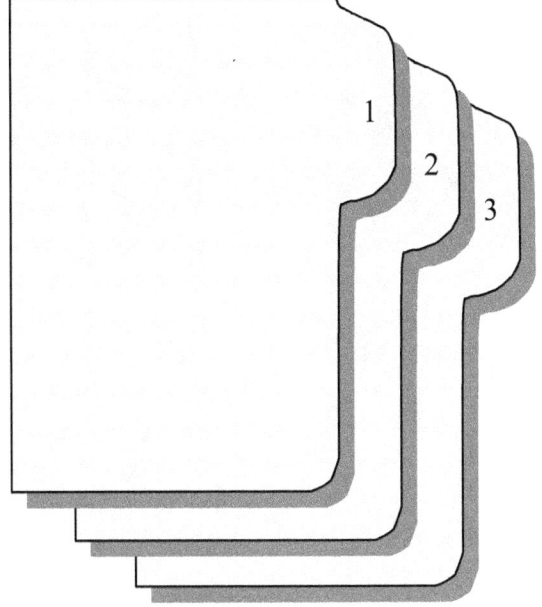

FIGURE 7-10. TABBING CORRESPONDENCE PACKAGES

THIS PAGE INTENTIONALLY LEFT BLANK

CHAPTER 8
Multiple-Address Letter

8-1 <u>General</u>. Use a multiple-address letter when you have more than one action addressee. The multiple-address letter is the same as the standard letter, except in handling addresses. Separate standard letters may be used in place of a multiple-address letter, but they require much more work.

8-2 <u>Listing Addresses</u>. There are three ways to list addresses:

1. <u>Using a "To:" Line Only</u>. When you have four addresses or fewer, use the "To:" line by itself as shown in figure 8-1.

2. <u>Using a "Distribution:" Line Only</u>. When you have more than four addresses, use the "Distribution:" line by itself as shown in figure 8-2.

3. <u>Using Both a "To:" Line and "Distribution:" Line</u>. Use both the "To:" line and the "Distribution:" line in the same letter when you show a group title whose distribution is relatively unknown. Place the group title ("Area Records Officers," for example) in the "To:" line and identify each member in a "Distribution:" line. See figure 8-3.

8-3 <u>Preparing and Signing Copies</u>. Every action addressee must receive a letter that has a letterhead and signature. The letterhead may be printed, typed, stamped, or photocopied. The signature must be original or photocopied. To meet these requirements, make copies in one of three ways.

1. Type original on letterhead paper. After the original has been signed, make the necessary photocopies. Keep the original signed copy in the official file and send out photocopies.

2. Using letterhead carbons, type all the copies needed for addresses and for the file if a single typing action will make them all. Then obtain an original signature on each action addressee's copy.

3. Using a word processor, type multiple originals on letterhead paper. Obtain an original signature on each action addressee's copy.

8-4 <u>Assembly of Multiple-Address Letters</u>. Figure 8-4 shows a suggested way to assemble a multiple-address letter for signature and mailing.

DEPARTMENT OF THE NAVY
COMMANDER SUBMARINE GROUP TWO
NAVAL SUBMARINE BASE NEW LONDON
GROTON, CONNECTICUT 06349-5100

```
                                              5216
                                              Ser N3/258
                                              25 Nov 09

From:   Commander, Submarine Group TWO
To:     Commander, Submarine Squadron TWO
        Commander, Submarine Squadron FOUR
        Commander, Submarine Squadron TWELVE

Subj:   USING A "TO:" LINE ONLY

1.  If you have four addressees or fewer, list all of them
in the "To:" line, starting one beneath the other.  If you
have more than four addressees, list all of them in a
"Distribution:" lines as shown on the next page.

2.  Use only long titles in the "To:" line.



                                    M. D. FOSTER
                                    By direction

Copy to:
COMNAVSEASYSCOM (SEA-06)
```

FIGURE 8-1. MULTIPLE-ADDRESS LETTER USING "TO:" LINE

DEPARTMENT OF THE NAVY
COMMANDER SUBMARINE GROUP TWO
NAVAL SUBMARINE BASE NEW LONDON
GROTON, CONNECTICUT 06349-5100

```
                                      5216
                                      Ser N3/260
                                      28 Nov 08
```

From: Commander, Submarine Group TWO

Subj: USING A "DISTRIBUTION:" LINE ONLY

1. Omit the "To:" line and add a "Distribution:" line if
you have more than four action addressees or if you vary
the number of copies to any of the addressees. Addressees
shown in a "Distribution:" line are action addressees.

2. You may list addressees in the "Distribution:" line
by:

    a. SNDL short titles

    b. Collective titles, or

    c. Both collective and SNDL short title.

3. Usually list "Distribution:" and "Copy to:" addressees
in single columns. Addressees may be listed in paragraphs
or columns to keep a letter from going to another page.


```
                              M. D. FOSTER
                              By direction
```

```
Distribution:
SNDL    28K1 (COMSUBFOR NORFOLK) (4 copies)
        29B1 USS ENTERPRISE (CVN 65)
        29N1 USS SCRANTON (SSN 756)
        32DD2 USS FRANK CABLE (AS 40)

Copy to:
COMNAVSEASYSCOM (SEA-06)
```

FIGURE 8-2. MULTIPLE-ADDRESS LETTER USING "DISTRIBUTION:" LINE

DEPARTMENT OF THE NAVY
COMMANDER
NAVAL COMPUTER AND TELECOMMUNICATIONS COMMAND
4401 MASSACHUSETTS AVE, N W
WASHINGTON, DC 20394-5000

```
                                          5216
                                          Ser 00C/1760
                                          18 Dec 09

From:   Commander, Naval Computer and
        Telecommunications Command
To:     Standard of Conduct Coordinators

Subj:   USING A "TO:" LINE AND "DISTRIBUTION:" LINE

1.  Use both the "To:" line and "Distribution:" line in the
same letter when you show a group title whose distribution
is relatively unknown.  Place the group title in the "To:"
line and identify each member in a "Distribution:" line.



                             R. HENDERSON
                             By direction

Distribution:
NAVCOMTELSTA WASHINGTON DC
NAVCOMTELSTA PENSACOLA
NAVCOMTELSTA SAN DIEGO
NAVCOMTELSTA SAN FRANCISCO
```

FIGURE 8-3. MULTIPLE-ADDRESS LETTER USING A "TO:" LINE AND
"DISTRIBUTION:" LINE

Here is a suggested way to assemble a multiple-address Letter for signature and mailing. If you use a folder rather than the single stack of papers shown, clip items 1 and 9 to the left side and 2 through 8 to the right side of the folder.

Tab signature page, enclosures, and background material.

Check or arrow the intended addressee on each copy.

Prepare envelopes or mailing labels according to local practice. Your activity might not require them for addressees listed in the SNDL.

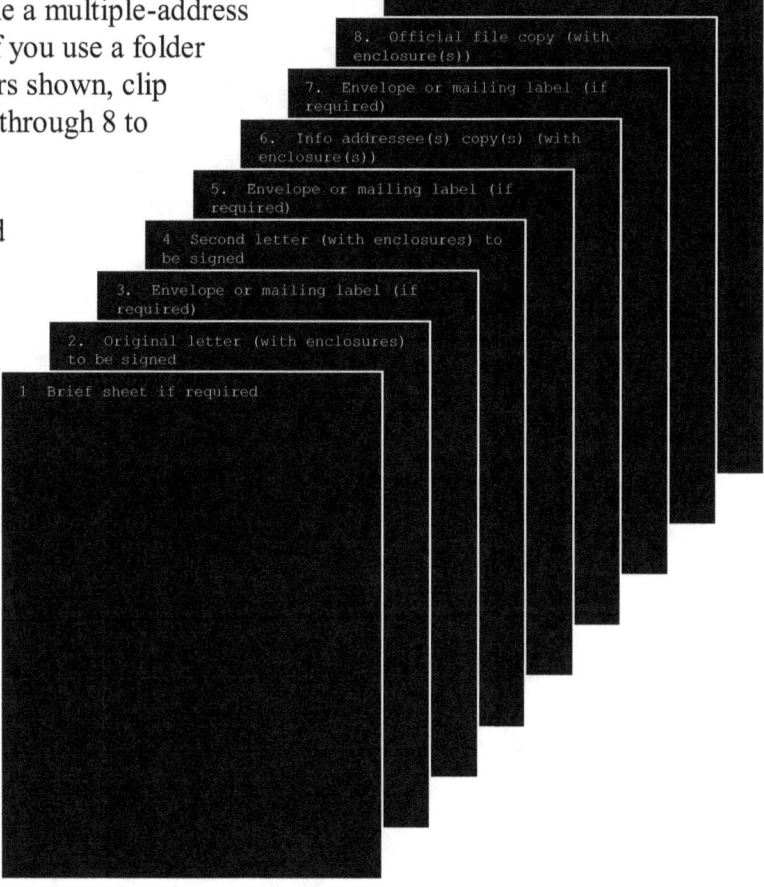

BEFORE SIGNATURE

1. Briefing sheet as prescribed locally, usually omitted if letter is short or self-explanatory.
2. Original letter to be signed (signature tabbed if not on first page), pages in normal order, with enclosures.
3. Envelope or mailing label, if required.
4. Second letter to be signed (signature tabbed if not on first page), pages in normal order, with enclosures.
5. Envelope or mailing label, if required.
6. Copies for "Copy to:" addressees, each with enclosures.
7. Envelope or mailing label, if required.
8. Official file copy of letter with enclosures. Expose the left margin so reviewers can initial and date there.
9. Background material.

AFTER SIGNATURE

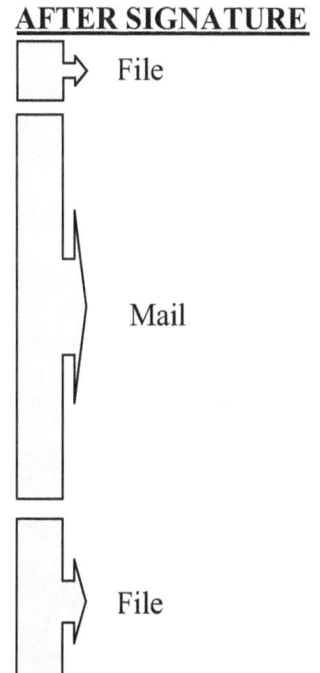

File

Mail

File

FIGURE 8-4. ASSEMBLY OF A MULTIPLE-ADDRESS LETTER

THIS PAGE INTENTIONALLY LEFT BLANK

CHAPTER 9
Endorsements

9-1 **General**. When a letter is transmitted via your activity, use an endorsement to forward comments, recommendations, or information. See figure 9-1. While an endorsement is mostly used to transmit correspondence through the chain of command, you may also use it to redirect a letter. Do not use an endorsement to reply to a routine letter. Additionally, a "Via" addressee may alter the order of any remaining "Via" addressees or add others.

9-2 **Format**

1. Endorsement Line

    a. Start the endorsement line at the left margin on the second line below the date line. If the correspondence is classified, start the endorsement line on the second line below the classification line.

    b. Number each endorsement in the sequence in which it is added to the basic letter. Indicate the numbers of the endorsement by using ordinal numbers such as FIRST, SECOND, THIRD, etc. Following the number, type "ENDORSEMENT on" and identify the basic letter using the same style as a reference line. When the heading exceeds one line, start the succeeding line with the word on.

Example:

FIRST ENDORSEMENT on USS SCRANTON (SSN 756) ltr 3000 Ser SSN 756/001 of
        5 May 96

2. "Via:" Line. When preparing your endorsement, include in the "Via:" line any remaining "Via" addressees, if any. If there is only one via addressee remaining do not number it. If there is more than one remaining, number the remaining addresses starting with the number (1) in parenthesis and consecutively number the rest.

3. Adding References. Do not repeat a reference in the reference line of your endorsement that has already been identified in the reference lines of the basic letter or a previous endorsement. Identify only the references that you add. Assign a letter to all references you add by continuing the sequence of letters from the basic letter and previous endorsements. For example, if the basic letter and previous endorsements had references identified up to letter "f," the first reference of your endorsement would be letter "g."

4. Adding Enclosures. Do not repeat an enclosure in your enclosure line that has already been identified in the enclosure lines of the basic letter or prior endorsements. Identify only the enclosures that you add. Assign a number to all enclosures that you add by continuing the sequence of numbers from the basic letter and previous endorsements. For example, if the basic letter and previous endorsements had enclosures identified up to number "5," the first enclosure of your endorsement would be number "6."

5. "Copy To:" Addressees. If your endorsement is significant and not routine, each activity that endorsed the basic letter before you and the originator of the basic letter shall be included as a copy to addressee on your endorsement. Additionally, all copy to addressees from the basic letter and previous endorsements shall be included as a copy to addressee. Significant endorsements include "forwarded, recommending disapproval," "readdressed and forwarded," and those with substantive comments. Routine endorsements include "forwarded," "forwarded for consideration," and "forwarded, recommending approval."

6. Forwarding Your Endorsement and Copies. When forwarding your endorsement to the next via addressee or to the action addressee, you must also do the following:

    a.   Attach any enclosure you identified in your endorsement to the original for forwarding to the action addressee.

    b.   Forward one copy of your endorsement to each remaining addressee.

    c.   Forward one copy of your endorsement to each copy to addressee. Include a copy of any enclosure you added. If a copy to addressee will be receiving the basic letter and previous endorsements for the first time from you, to the right of each of these addressees, type the word "complete" in parentheses to show that your endorsement includes the basic letter, enclosures, and prior endorsements.

7. Assembly of an Endorsement. Figure 9-2 shows a suggested way to assemble an endorsement for signature and mailing.

DEPARTMENT OF THE NAVY
NAVAL AIR FORCE ATLANTIC
1279 FRANKLIN STREET
NORFOLK VA 23511-2494

5216
Ser N72/420
24 Jul 06

%
SECOND ENDORSEMENT on NAS Cecil Field ltr 5216 Ser 11/273
*******************of 9 Jul 06
%
From:**Commander, Naval Air Force, U.S. Atlantic Fleet
To:****Commander, U.S. Atlantic Fleet
%
Subj:**HOW TO PREPARE AN ENDORSEMENT
%
Encl:**(2)*SECNAV M-5216.5
%
1.**Start an endorsement on a new page. Number each page of
your endorsement and continue the sequence of numbers from the
previous endorsement or from the basic letter if you are the
first endorser.
%
2.**Every "new page" endorsement must repeat the basic
letter's SSIC, identify the basic letter in the endorsement
line, and use the basic letter's subject as its own.
%
%
%

                         J. H. KNIGHT
                         By direction

%
Copy to:
NAS Cecil Field (Code 11)
*COMSEABASEDASWWINGLANT (Code 019)

***Prior endorser included because second endorsement is
significant.**

4

FIGURE 9-1. NEW PAGE ENDORSEMENT

This is a suggested method to way to assemble an endorsement for signature and mailing. If you use a folder rather than the single stack of papers shown, clip items 1 and 11 to the left side and 2 through 10 to the right side of the folder.

Tab signature page, enclosures, and background material.

Check or arrow the intended addressee on each copy.

Prepare envelopes or mailing labels according to local practice. Your activity might not require them for addressees listed in the SNDL.

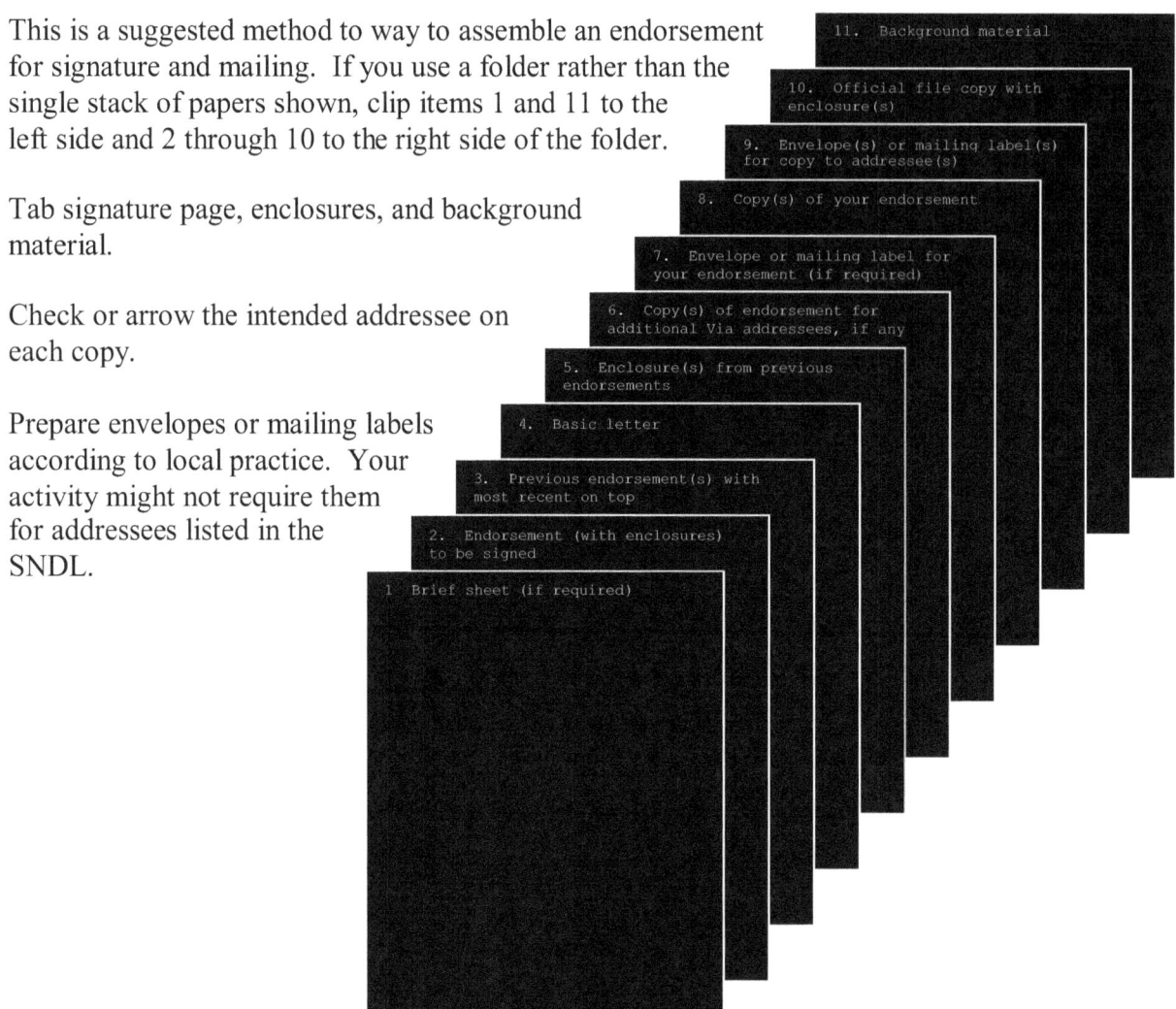

11. Background material

10. Official file copy with enclosure(s)

9. Envelope(s) or mailing label(s) for copy to addressee(s)

8. Copy(s) of your endorsement

7. Envelope or mailing label for your endorsement (if required)

6. Copy(s) of endorsement for additional Via addressees, if any

5. Enclosure(s) from previous endorsements

4. Basic letter

3. Previous endorsement(s) with most recent on top

2. Endorsement (with enclosures) to be signed

1. Brief sheet (if required)

BEFORE SIGNATURE

1. Briefing sheet as prescribed locally, usually omitted if letter is short or self explanatory.

2. Your endorsement.

3. Earlier endorsements, most recent on top.

4. Basic letter.

5. Earlier enclosures, plus any you added on top.

6. Copies of your endorsement for remaining Via addressees.

7. Envelope or mailing label, if required.

8. Copies of your endorsement for copy to addressees.

9. Envelope or mailing label, if required.

10. Official file copy of letter with enclosures. Left margin exposed so reviewers can initial and date there.

11. Background material, such as incoming letter, referenced documents.

AFTER SIGNATURE

File

Mail to next via addressee or to the action addressee

Mail

File

FIGURE 9-2. ASSEMBLY OF AN ENDORSEMENT

CHAPTER 10
Memorandums

10-1 **General**. A memorandum provides a less formal way to correspond within an activity/command. Subordinates within that activity or command may use a memorandum to correspond directly with each other on routine official business or as an informal means of communication.

10-2 **Formats**. There are several memorandum formats. All DON activities shall use the appropriate memorandum that suits the subject, occasion, and audience. The following paragraphs discuss the different types of memorandums:

1. Memorandum For The Record. Use a Memorandum for the Record (MFR) as an internal document to record supporting information in the record that is not recorded elsewhere. Examples include such things as documenting the results of a meeting, an important telephone conversation, or an oral agreement. Type or handwrite these most informal memorandums. See figure 10-1. A full signature line and identification symbols are not required; however, it should be dated, signed, and show the organizational position of the signer. If it is only two or three lines, include it on the file copy of your document. Leave out the subject line if you add your MFR to the file copy.

2. From-To Memorandum. Use OPNAV 5215/144A DON Memo (8-1/2 X 11) or OPNAV 5215/144B DON Memo (8-1/5 X 5-1/2) for the "from—to" memorandum. Memorandum may be directed to one or more addressees. If very informal, it may be handwritten. If the subject is insignificant, a file copy is not required. See figure 10-2.

3. Plain-Paper Memorandum. Use plain-paper memorandums for informal communications within your activity. It is no more formal than the memorandum form, but it is more flexible when there are multiple addressees, via addressees, or both.

   a. Identification Symbols. The only identification symbol you need is the date, unless local practice calls for more.

   b. Format. Prepare on white bond paper. Type the date on the sixth line so it ends flush with the right margin unless it is used as part of the senders symbol. See figures 10-3 and 10-4.

4. Letterhead Memorandum. The letterhead memorandum may be used within your activity and provides more formality than the printed form or plain-paper memorandum. When direct liaison with individuals outside of your activity is authorized, the letterhead memorandum may be used to correspond on routine matters that neither make a commitment nor take an official stand. A full signature line is not required because the "From:" line identifies the signer. See figure 10-4. For example: You have been appointed chairperson of a committee and need to correspond with other members of the committee outside your activity.

5. <u>Decision Memorandum</u>. When only requesting an approval/disapproval decision from a single addressee, it is appropriate to type a decision block at the left margin, two lines below the signature line in the following format:

COMMANDING OFFICER DECISION:

_____ Approved

_____ Disapproved

_____ Other

6. <u>Memorandum of Agreement or Memorandum of Understanding</u>

   a. <u>Use</u>. The Memorandum of Agreement or Understanding may be used to document mutual agreements of facts, intentions, procedures, limits on future actions, and areas of present or future coordination, or commitments, etc. If a Memorandum of Agreement or Understanding is initiated by a non-DoD activity, DON activities are authorized to use their format.

   b. <u>Format</u>. Center "MEMORANDUM OF AGREEMENT" on the second line below the date line. Center "BETWEEN" on the next line and follow with the names of the agreeing activities (centered). To prepare a "Memorandum of Understanding," substitute those words for "Memorandum of Agreement," and follow the same format as shown in figures 10-5 and 10-16. Number and letter paragraphs and subparagraphs the same as other correspondence. The basic text may contain, but is not limited to, the following titled paragraphs:

      (1) <u>Purpose</u>. This paragraph defines or states in as few words as possible, the purpose of the agreement.

      (2) <u>Problem</u>. Present a clear, concise statement of the problem, to include a brief background.

      (3) <u>Scope</u>. Add a short statement specifying the area covered by the agreement.

      (4) <u>Agreement, Understanding</u>. Spell out the agreement or understanding and responsibilities of and between each of the parties involved.

      (5) <u>Effective Date</u>. Enter the date the agreement will take effect.

   c. <u>Letterhead</u>. On plain bond, type the command titles so the senior is at the top. If the activities are in different cities or states, follow each title with its address.

   d. <u>Signatures</u>. Arrange signature lines so the senior official is at the right. Place the signature line of a third cosigner in the middle of the page. Precede all signature lines by over scoring as shown in figures 10-5 and 10-7. The senior activity should sign the agreement after the junior activity(ies).

   e. <u>Copies</u>. The activity signing last should send copies of the agreement to all cosigners.

```
                                          17 Jun 09
%
MEMORANDUM FOR THE RECORD
%
Subj:**MEMORANDUM FOR THE RECORD
%
1.**Use an MFR to record information in the record
that is not recorded elsewhere.  Examples include such
things as results of a meeting, telephone
conversations, oral agreements, and other relevant
information.
%
2.**Type or handwrite these most informal memorandums.
If it is only two or three lines, include it on the
file copy of your document.  Leave out the subject
line if you add your MFR to the file copy.
%
3.**A full signature line and identification symbols
are not required; however, it should be dated, signed,
and show the signer's organizational code.
%
%
%
                         M. J. FORD
                         N11
```

FIGURE 10-1. MEMORANDUM FOR THE RECORD

SAMPLE

DEPARTMENT OF THE NAVY
Memorandum

DATE:

FROM:

TO:

SUBJ:
----------------The area above this line is preprinted. Fill in as appropriate.--------------
%
Ref:***(a)*SECNAV M-5216.1
%
Encl:**(1)*Printed Form
%
1.**This printed form is used for corresponding between
individuals and offices of the same activity. Very informal
memorandums may be hand written.
%
2.**The memorandum form comes in two sizes:
%
****a.**OPNAV 5216/144A (8-1/2 by 11 inches):
%
****b.**OPNAV 5216/144B (8-1/2 by 5-1/2 inches):
%
3.**The only identification symbol you need is the date, unless
local practice calls for more.
%
4.**Use names, titles, or codes in the "From:" and "To:" lines.
%
5.**Type reference and enclosure headings under the printed
headings. Note the headings for reference (a) and enclosure
(1). Allow a 1-inch left margin.
%
6.**The writer signs his or her name without the organizational
titles.
%
%
%

                              Signature

OPNAV 5216/144A (Rev. AUG 1981)

FIGURE 10-2. PRINTED "FROM-TO" MEMORANDUM

```
%
%
%
%
%
                                                    8 Jul 09

%
MEMORANDUM
%
From:**Head, DON Records Management Branch (N161)
To:****Head, Technical Library Branch (N21)
******Head, Mail and Files Branch (N13)
Via:***Head, Office Services Division (N1)
%
Subj:**PLAIN-PAPER MEMORANDUM
%
1.**The plain-paper "from-to" memorandum may be used within
your activity.  It is no more formal than the memorandum
form, but it is more flexible when there are multiple
addressees, via addressees, or both.
%
2.**The only identification symbol you need is the date,
unless local practice calls for more.  Start typing the date
on the sixth line, flush with the right margin.
%
3.**Prepare a plain-paper memorandum on white bond.
%
%
%

                        N. D. SOLAR
```

FIGURE 10-3. PLAIN-PAPER "FROM-TO" MEMORANDUM

DEPARTMENT OF THE NAVY
NAVAL AIR FORCE
U.S. ATLANTIC FLEET
NORFOLK VA 22015-3421

5216
Memo 00/83
5 Jan 10

%
MEMORANDUM
%
From:**Head, Management Services Department, Naval
*******Air Facility, Detroit
To:****Operations Officer, Navy Regional Data
*******Automation Center, San Francisco
%
Subj:**LETTERHEAD MEMORANDUM
%
1.**When used within an activity, the letterhead memorandum
provides more formality than the printed memorandum form or
the plain-paper memorandum.
%
2.**A letterhead memorandum may be sent outside your
activity if:
%
****a.**Direct liaison is authorized,
%
****b.**The matter is routine, and
%
****c.**The memo neither makes a commitment nor takes an
official stand.
%
3.**Generally follow the standard letter format, but type
"MEMORANDUM" as shown here.
%
%
%

W. S. NELSON

FIGURE 10-4. LETTERHEAD MEMORANDUM

```
                    DEPARTMENT OF THE NAVY
                   NAVAL AIR FORCE ATLANTIC
                   NORFOLK VA 23511-2494
%
MSC                                              NAVINTCOM
5216                                             5216
Ser N02/234                                      Ser N7/702
18 Dec 09                                        20 Dec 09
%
                   MEMORANDUM OF AGREEMENT
                           BETWEEN
            COMMANDER, MILITARY SEALIFT COMMAND
                             AND
            COMMANDER, NAVAL INTELLIGENCE COMMAND
%
Subj:**MEMORANDUM OF AGREEMENT
%
1.**This example shows a one page "Memorandum of Agreement"
(MOA).
%
2.**On plain bond, type the command titles so the senior is
at the top.  If the activities are in different cities or
states, follow each title with its address.
%
3.**Center "MEMORANDUM OF AGREEMENT" on the second line
below the date line.  Center "BETWEEN" on the next line and
follow with the names of the agreeing activities.  To
prepare a "Memorandum of Understanding" substitute those
words for "Memorandum of Agreement."  If your agreement is
two or more pages long, number and letter paragraphs and
subparagraphs the same as a standard letter.
%
4.**Arrange signature lines so the senior official is at the
right.  Type a signature line above the signature lines.
%
5.**If your activity is the last to sign, send copies of the
signed agreement to all cosigners.
%
%
%


_____            _____
M. L. SIMPSON                B. D. WATSON
Acting                       Deputy
```

FIGURE 10-5. MEMORANDUM OF AGREEMENT

```
                    DEPARTMENT OF THE NAVY
                    NAVAL AIR FORCE ATLANTIC
                    NORFOLK VA 23511-2494
%
NAVSEASYSCOM                              NAVAIRSYSCOM
5216                                     5216
Ser N02/234                             Ser N7/702
12 Nov 09                               15 Nov 09
%
                 MEMORANDUM OF UNDERSTANDING
                          BETWEEN
          COMMANDER, NAVAL SEA SYSTEMS COMMAND
                            AND
          COMMANDER, NAVAL AIR SYSTEMS COMMAND
%
Subj:**MEMORANDUM OF UNDERSTANDING
%
Ref:***(a) SECNAV M-5216.5
%
1.**Purpose.  This example shows the first page of a two-
page "Memorandum of Understanding" (MOU).  This paragraph
defines or states, in as few words as possible, the purpose
of the agreement or understanding.  Use the MOU or MOA to
informally document mutual agreements of:
%
****a.**Facts.
%
****b.**Intentions.
%
****c.**Procedures.
%
****d.**Limits of future actions either or both will take.
%
****e.**Present or future coordination.
%
****f.**Present or future commitments.
%
2.**Problem.**Present a clear, concise statement of the
problem, to include a brief background.  Mention reference
(a) and any other references in the text.
%
3.**Scope.**Add a short statement specifying the area
covered by the agreement.
```

FIGURE 10-6. MEMORANDUM OF UNDERSTANDING – FIRST PAGE

```
Subj:**MEMORANDUM OF UNDERSTANDING
%
4.**Agreement/Understanding.  Spell out the agreement or
understanding and responsibilities of and between each of
the parties involved.
%
5.**Effective Date.  Enter the date the agreement will take
effect.
%
%
%
_____            _____
W. T. DOOR                  T. CRUISE
                            Acting
```

2

FIGURE 10-7. MEMORANDUM OF UNDERSTANDING - SECOND PAGE

THIS PAGE INTENTIONALLY LEFT BLANK

CHAPTER 11
Business Letters

11-1 **General**. Use the business letter to correspond with agencies, businesses, or individuals outside DoD, who are unfamiliar with the standard letter. It also may be used for official correspondence between individuals within DoD, when the occasion calls for a personal approach. Before reading further, review figures 11-1, 11-2, and 11-3.

11-2 **Parts of a Business Letter and Format**

1. Identification Symbols. Include the following three identification symbols in the upper left corner, blocked one below the other:

    a. SSIC;

    b. Originator's code; and

    c. Date. Write the date in month-day-year order. The month is written out in full, followed by the day in Arabic numerals, a comma, and the full year also in Arabic numerals, e.g., May 25, 1967.

2. Inside Address. Place the inside address two to eight lines below the date, blocked flush with the left margin. Placement of the inside address may be adjusted depending on the length of the letter or local policy. Refer to figure 11-4 for proper placement of the inside address when preparing a letter for use with a window envelope.

    a. If your letter is directed to a particular individual, include the:

        (1) Addressee's courtesy title (Mr., Mrs., Ms.) and full name;

        (2) business title (Vice President, Accounting), if appropriate;

        (3) business name;

        (4) street address; and

        (5) the city, state, and ZIP+4 code on the last line. Note new requirement for only one space between state and ZIP code vice two to five spaces.

    b. If your letter is directed to a business in general, include the:

        (1) Business name;

        (2) full street address; and

        (3) the city, state, and ZIP+4 code on the last line.

3.   Attention Line. An attention line is optional. Use it to direct your letter to a business in general and to also bring it to the attention of a particular person or department at the same time. Start typing two lines below the last line of the inside address, blocked flush with the left margin, and two lines above the salutation. See figure 11-5. Refer to figure 11-4 for proper placement of the attention line when preparing a letter for use with a window envelope.

4.   Salutation Line. Capitalize the first letter of the first word of the salutation as well as the first letter of the addressee's courtesy title and surname such as "Dear Mr. (or Ms., Mrs., Miss, Dr., Captain, Lieutenant) Jones," followed by a colon.

    a.   If your letter is addressed to:

       (1)   An all male organization, use a salutation such as "Gentlemen" or "Dear Sirs."

       (2)   An all female organization, use a salutation such as "Ladies" or "Mesdames."

       (3)   A mixed gender organization, or if you are not sure of the gender mix, use a collective salutation such as "Ladies and Gentlemen" or "Dear Sir or Madam."

       (4)   A business in general, but directed to the attention of a particular person or department, use a collective salutation such as "Ladies and Gentlemen."

    b.   If you cannot determine the gender of the addressee from previous communications, omit the courtesy title (Mr., Mrs., Ms., etc.) and address the individual by first name or initial(s) and last name such as "Dear Lee Doe" or "Dear L. Doe."

    c.   Refer to appendices A and B for models of address and salutations. Start typing on the second line below the last line of the inside address or attention line, flush with the left margin.

5.   Subject Line. Use of a subject line is optional and may replace the salutation. The subject line should be very brief, to the point, and not be more than one line in length if possible. Capitalize every letter in the subject line. See figure 11-2.

    a.   If the subject line is replacing the salutation, start typing on the second line below the last line of the inside address or attention line, flush with the left margin.

    b.   If the subject line is in addition to the salutation, start typing on the second line below the salutation line.

6.   Body of the Letter. Single-space within paragraphs and double space between paragraphs. Indent main paragraphs four spaces and start typing on the fifth space. Do not number main paragraphs. The first lines of subparagraphs should be indented, and lettered or numbered in standard letter fashion. See figure 11-1. A business letter that is likely to run eight lines or less may be double-spaced. Figure 11-6 is an illustration of a short business letter.

7. References and Enclosures. Refer to previous communications and enclosures in the body of the letter only, without calling them references or enclosures.

8. Complimentary Close. Use "Sincerely" followed by a comma for the complimentary close of a business letter starting at the center of the page on the second line below the text.

9. Signature Line

 a. Start all lines of the signature line at the center of the page, beginning on the fourth line below "Sincerely." Type or stamp the following information:

 (1) Signer's name in all capital letters, with the exception of a last name starting with a prefix, which would appear like this:

EXAMPLE:

                              J. A. McBREARTY

 (2) Military grade (if any) spelled out,

 (3) Functional title, and

 (4) Authority line. The authority line may be omitted on a routine business letter that neither makes a commitment nor takes an official stand.

 b. Women's names may begin with "Miss," "Mrs.," or "Ms." One exception to this would be when using "Mrs." plus the writer's husband's name, which would appear like this: "MS. ALBERT B. SEAY" or "MRS. A. B. SEAY."

10. Enclosure Line

 a. Type "Enclosure" on the second line below the signature line, number and describe them briefly.

EXAMPLE:

Enclosures: 1. GPO Style Manual
             2. Webster's Dictionary

 b. If the enclosures are insignificant, you do not have to describe them in the enclosure line. Type "Enclosures" and the number of enclosures within parentheses: Enclosures (2).

11. Separate Mailing. When an enclosure is to be sent separately, type "Separate Mailing" and a brief description like this:

EXAMPLE:

Separate Mailing: SECNAV M-5216.5

12. "Copy To:" Line. If everyone should know that a particular addressee will receive an information copy, show that addressee by using a copy notation. Type "Copy to:" at the left margin on the second line below the enclosure line, if any, or the signature line. List addressees at the left margin or following "Copy to:". Use long titles for activities listed in the SNDL:

EXAMPLE:

Copy to: Chief of Naval Operations (N86)

13. Outgoing Copies. Because the business letter does not have a "From:" line, every copy that goes to addressees outside your activity must have a letterhead copy (printed, typed, stamped, or reproduced from the original) to show its origin.

14. Identifying Second and Succeeding Pages. Repeat the identification symbols, from the first page, on the sixth line from the top at the left margin. Continue the text beginning on the second line below the identification symbols. See figure 11-3.

15. Numbering Pages. Do not number a single-page letter or the first page of a multiple-page letter. Center page numbers 1/2 inch from the bottom edge, starting with the number 2. No punctuation accompanies a page number. (To number the pages of a Top Secret document, see SECNAV M-5510.36.)

```
****Main paragraph format.
%
********a.**Indent each new subdivision eight spaces
and start typing at the ninth space.
%
********b.**Text.
%
***********(1)*Documents rarely require subdividing to
the extent shown below.
%
***********(2)*Text.
%
**************(a)*Text.
%
**************(b)*Text.
%
*****************(1)*Text.
%
*****************(2)*Text.
%
********************(a)*Text.
%
********************(b)*Never subparagraph beyond
this level.
%
****Text.
%
********a.**Indent each new subdivision eight spaces
and start typing at the ninth space.
%
********b.**Text.
%
***********(9)*Text.
%
***********(10)*When using two digits, continue to
indent each new subdivision (paragraphs will not line
up).
```

FIGURE 11-1. BUSINESS LETTER PARAGRAPH FORMATS

DEPARTMENT OF THE NAVY
USS NEW HAMPSHIRE (SSN 778)
FPO AE 09579-2305

                                        5216
                                        Ser SSN 778/28
                                        January 5, 2009

%
Mr. A. B. Seay
Vice President, Accounting
Widgets Unlimited, Inc.
1234 Any Street
Baltimore, MD 21085-1234
%
Dear Mr. Seay:
%
SUBJECT: PREPARATION OF A BUSINESS LETTER
%
****This example shows the first page of a two-page
business letter. A subject line is optional, but if used
will replace the salutation. Phrase the subject line in
normal word order. Make it very brief, to the point, and
not longer than one line. Capitalize every letter in the
subject line.
%
****Refer to previous communications and enclosures in the
body of the letter only, without calling them references or
enclosures. Do not number main paragraphs. Subparagraphs
are numbered and lettered the same as a standard letter.
%
****Start a paragraph near the end of a page only if that
page has room for two lines or more. Continue a paragraph
on the following page only if two lines or more can be
carried over. A signature page must have at least two
lines of text.
%
****Do not number the first page of a single page letter or
multiple page letter. The first page is assumed to be page
1. Center page numbers 1/2 inch from the bottom edge,
starting with the number 2. No punctuation accompanies a
page number.

FIGURE 11-2. BUSINESS LETTER – FIRST PAGE

```
                                        5216
                                        Ser SSN 778/28
                                        January 5, 2009
%
****This example illustrates second and final page of a
business letter.  Start typing on the sixth line flush with
the left margin.  Repeat sender symbol from the first page.
Continue the text from the first page on the second line
below the date.
%
****Be sure to mention any enclosed documents in the body
of your letter and list them as enclosures on the second
line below the signature line.  Type "Enclosures:" and
follow with a number and a brief description of the
enclosures (do not number when you have only one
enclosure).  When the enclosures are of little importance,
instead of listing them with a description, you may
indicate the number of enclosures in parentheses without
the description; e.g., Enclosures (2).  Materials, referred
to in the letter, that are being mailed separately should
be noted as shown below.
%
****To send an addressee an information copy or a courtesy
copy, type "Copy to:" flush with the left margin, two lines
below the signature line or two lines below any preceding
notation, such as the enclosure or separate mailing
notation.
%
                         Sincerely,
%
%
%

                         R. TREVOR KING
                         Executive Officer
                         By direction
                         of the Commander
%
Enclosures:**1.**Sample Business Letter
************2.**SECNAVINST 5216.50
%
Separate Mailing:**Secretarial Handbook
%
Copy to:**Chief of Naval Operations (N61)
```

2

FIGURE 11-3. BUSINESS LETTER - SECOND PAGE

DEPARTMENT OF THE NAVY
USS MOMSEN (DDG 92)
FPO AP 99672–1307

5216
Ser 303/405
June 8, 2009

Line 16   ATTN: RECORDS MANAGER
C & A TOOL COMPANY
505 FRANKLIN STREET
BELVIEW, VA 22812-1234

Line 25   SUBJECT: SUBJECT LINE AND WINDOW-ENVELOPE FORMAT

[C & A Tool Company,] In this example the subject line
is used in place of the salutation. This is allowed on
routine administrative letters. The first sentence serves
as a greeting to the reader as shown above in [ ]. Start
typing the identification symbols on line 10, just below
the seal. Always start the address on line 16; the
salutation or subject line on line 25.

You may use a number 10 window envelope if the entire
address takes no more than five lines, it does not extend
past the middle of the page, and the letter and all
enclosures are unclassified. The full address must appear
in the window no matter how the letter may shift in the
envelope.

To fold the letter, turn up the bottom edge so it just
covers the subject and then turn back the address portion
so the upper fold falls along the top of the subject.

Sincerely,

ANN C. PHILLIPS
Commander, U.S. Navy
Executive Officer
By direction of the
Commanding Officer

FIGURE 11-4. BUSINESS LETTER FOR WINDOW ENVELOPES

DEPARTMENT OF THE NAVY
USS ENTERPRISE (CVN 65)
FPO AE 09543-2810

```
                                        5216
                                        Ser 945/321
                                        June 7, 2006
```

%

National Widget Company
6543 W. Hobson Street
New York, NY 12345-6789

%

Attention: H. Jones

%

Ladies and Gentlemen:

%

****When writing to a company, but directing your letter to a
particular person or office, use an attention line. The
attention line is placed two lines below the last line of the
inside address; type "Attention:" and then a name or title.

%

****The salutation must agree with the first line of the
address. It the first line is a business, division, or
organization collectively, a collective salutation such as
"Ladies and Gentlemen" is used even if the attention line
directs the letter to an individual. Note the inside address
and salutation in this letter.

```
                              Sincerely,



                              S. F. HANSON
                              Commander, U.S. Navy
                              Commanding Officer
                              Acting
```

FIGURE 11-5. BUSINESS LETTER WITH AN "ATTENTION" LINE

DEPARTMENT OF THE NAVY
OFFICE OF THE CHIEF OF NAVAL OPERATIONS
2000 NAVY PENTAGON
WASHINGTON DC 20350-2000

5216
Ser 301/789
April 7, 2006

%
Ms. Jane Ryan
J. M. Corporation
287 Duke Street
Newton, CA 93333-4321
%
Dear Ms. Ryan:
%
****This is an illustration of a short business letter.
There are several techniques you may use to balance the
appearance of a letter containing 100 words or less:
%
****a.**Start the inside address up to eight lines below
the date.
%
****b.**Use side margins of up to two inches.
%
****c.**In a letter containing eight lines or less, you
may double-space throughout the text.

{Note proper use of Ms. in parentheses in signature line.}
%
                                    Sincerely,

%

%

%

                              (Ms.) F. E. ROBINSON
                              Head, Management Services

FIGURE 11-6. SHORT BUSINESS LETTER

CHAPTER 12
Executive Correspondence

12-1 **General**. This section provides specific guidance on the internal and external written communication particular to the Headquarters, Department of the Navy (HqDON). When forwarding correspondence to offices of flag/general officers and senior civilian officials within HqDON, every effort should be made to strictly adhere to prescribed formats, as deviation could unnecessarily delay processing for administrative action or complete restaffing.

12-2 **Processes**

1. Correspondence Management. HqDON correspondence is safeguarded and electronically routed, reviewed, and edited through the Correspondence Management System – Taskers Version 4.4. Taskers is a Web-based computer tracking system that is utilized as a contexts manager for all official action and information correspondence (referred to as "taskers") for HqDON and selected echelon 2 commands. Refer to the Tasker User Guide 2006 for detailed guidance on the Correspondence Management System.

2. Assigning Action to Incoming Correspondence. All action or information correspondence received in HqDON is analyzed and routed to the appropriate office by the tasking authority for chop, action, coordination or information.

   a. Office of the Secretary and Under Secretary of the Navy. All action or information correspondence for the Office of the Secretary of the Navy, Administrative Office (1000 Navy Pentagon, Room 4E652, Washington, DC 20350) is controlled, routed and safeguarded.

      (1) Incoming correspondence

         (a) Upon receipt, general and Congressional correspondence shall be routed to an executive civilian or staff assistant per SECNAVINST 5430.7Q, Assignment of Responsibilities and Authorities in the Office of the Secretary of the Navy, and assigned as the action office to facilitate coordination and review via SECNAV or Under Secretary of the Navy (UNSECNAV) signature.

         (b) Operational correspondence shall be assigned to the Director, Navy Staff or the Director, Marine Corps Staff, as appropriate, for action or coordination to prepare proposed responses for SECNAV or UNSECNAV signature.

         (c) When coordination is required by both Navy and Marine Corps, the Office of the Secretary of the Navy will determine who shall be the appropriate lead action office.

      (2) Outgoing correspondence

   b. Office of the Chief and Vice Chief of Naval Operations. All action or information correspondence for the CNO and Vice Chief of Naval Operations (VCNO) signature is controlled, routed and safeguarded by the Office of the Director, Navy Staff, Attn: Executive Secretary (2000 Navy Pentagon, Room 4E563, Washington DC 20350).

      (1) Incoming correspondence

      (2) Outgoing correspondence

    c.   Office of the Commandant and Assistant Commandant of the Marine Corps. All action or information correspondence for the CMC or Assistant Commandant of the Marine Corps (ACMC) signature is controlled, routed and safeguarded by the Office of the Director, Marine Corps Staff (3000 Marine Corps Pentagon, Room 4E448, Washington, DC 20350).

3.   Routing Changes. Changes to action office assignment shall be made within 48 hours of initial assignment. If the package requires transfer to another agency or office after that time, the original action office shall coordinate with the receiving office. Prior to transferring action, provide tasking authority with the name, organization, and telephone number of the new action office.

4.   Due Dates

    a.   General Correspondence. All general correspondence should be responded to within 20 working days of being entered into the Central Management System (CMS) for taskers. If additional time is required, an interim letter and/or an approved extension are mandatory.

    b.   Congressional Correspondence. All Congressional correspondence should be responded to within 7 working days of being entered into taskers. If additional time is required, an interim letter will be sent. A copy of the interim letter shall be forwarded to the SECNAV Congressional Liaison Office (CLO) for their files. All extensions must be coordinated with SECNAV CLO.

5.   Extensions. To request an extension of an OSD tasker, the action office must provide the necessary information and prepare an official extension request with a SD Form 391 Secretary of Defense Correspondence Action Report (see figure 12-1). The action office will also need to provide a copy of the proposed interim that will be sent to the correspondent. All documents shall be placed in the working documents area of the assigned tasker.

6.   Interims

    a.   HqDON Correspondence

      (1) An interim response shall be provided in the event the tasker cannot be answered within the allotted time. It shall be used to acknowledge receipt of the tasker or letter, but more importantly, to signal the desire to be responsive. The interim response will provide an overview of the information available; the reason for the delay, along with a reasonable anticipated date that the final reply shall be provided.

(2) It is the responsibility of the action office to ensure timely planning in the preparation of interim responses. There shall be no extensions given in order to complete an interim letter. The action office concerned shall forward a copy of all interim responses to SECNAV Admin for retention. Subsequent interims shall be approved by the Administrative Aide to the Secretary of the Navy (AASN).

b.   OSD Correspondence. An interim response shall be prepared in accordance with paragraph 6a. The interim response shall be signed out at the Assistant Secretary of the Navy (ASN) level.

c.   Congressional Correspondence. An interim response is required in the event the tasker cannot be answered within the allotted time. It shall be used to acknowledge receipt of the tasker or letter, but more importantly to signal the desire to be responsive (refer to figures 12-2, 12-3 and 12-4).

7.   Distribution

a.   A signed/dated copy of the correspondence with a copy of the action memo, references, and background materials shall be returned to the action office. Only a signed copy of the response shall be forwarded to the coordinating offices.

b.   Envelopes and labels for all correspondence are the responsibility of the action office and shall be included in all SECNAV/UNSECNAV or OSD signature packages. If packages are missing labels, completed and signed correspondence shall be returned to the action office for distribution.

12-3   **General Guidelines for Preparing a Letter**. Use letters for correspondence with individuals outside the U.S. Government and for formal correspondence with officials of other Federal agencies.

1.   Stationery. Prepare all outgoing correspondence for SECNAV, CNO, or designated official signature on the following letterhead:

a.   Use SECNAV flag stationery (refer to figures 12-7 and 12-8) for personal correspondence only (8 1/2 inches by 11 inches or 5 inches by 7 inches). Use plain bond for successive pages.

b.   Use SECNAV/UNSECNAV letterhead with DoD seal (refer to figures 12-2 and 12-3) for official correspondence (i.e., SECNAV addressed letters, business and personal, or official responses to outside government officials) letters and memorandums requiring the SECNAV or UNSECNAV signature). Use plain bond paper for successive pages. Additionally, use the DON, Office of the Secretary of the Navy (refer to figure 12-6) when authorized to sign on behalf of SECNAV (i.e., SECNAV instructions, notices and "reply direct" action responses).

c.   CNO

d.   VCNO

2. <u>Format</u>. Prepare all correspondence using 13 point, Times New Roman Font.

    a.   <u>Salutations</u>. All salutations shall be formal. The following guidance can be used to prepare salutations, text for the body of the letter, closing lines, complimentary close and signature line:

    b.   <u>Opening Lines</u>

        (1) "Thank you for your letter of (date – November 6, 2005 – only use date if response is timely) concerning…"

        (2) "Thank you for your recent letter(s) concerning………"

        (3) "I am responding on behalf of…"

    c.   <u>Body of the Letter</u>

        (1) Limit the use of "I" and "we."

        (2) Indent each paragraph five spaces, start typing on the sixth space and do not number the paragraphs.

        (3) Limit response to one page whenever possible. Use enclosures if necessary.

        (4) An acronym may be used after it is spelled out (be consistent throughout the document).

        (5) Spell out percent (instead of using the sign "%").

        (6) In replying to more than one member of Congress, you may use either:

            (a) "A similar response has been sent to Senator (last name) and Senator (last name), Congressman (last name) and Congressman (last name)."

            (b) "A similar response has been sent to each of your colleagues who also expressed an interest in this issue."

    d.   <u>Closing Lines</u> (last paragraph)

        (1) "Thank you for bringing this matter to my attention."

        (2) "I appreciate you taking the time to share your thoughts on this issue."

        (3) "As always, if I can be of any further assistance, please let me know." (Preferred on Congressional responses.)

e. <u>Signature Lines</u>

(1) Correspondence prepared for the signature of other officials should contain standard closing and signature lines.

(2) The following is a sample of the signature line:

(a) Type the name at the center of the page on fourth line below the last line of text or complimentary close.

(b) Type the official title on the line below his/her name commencing at the center of the page as well.

EXAMPLES:

Senior Civilian	Military

Ashley Godwin
Deputy Assistant Secretary of the Navy
   (Financial Management & Comptroller)
	C. W. MARTOGLIO
	Rear Admiral, U.S. Navy
	Senior Military Assistant
	   to the Secretary of the Navy

NOTE: Title/position is not required if reflected in the letterhead.

---

f. <u>Copy To</u>. When writing a member of Congress in the capacity of Committee Chairman, send a courtesy copy to the Committee ranking minority member (see figures 12-4, 12-5, and 12-6). Indicate the "Copy to" addressee at the bottom left of the letter (two lines after signature line).

EXAMPLE: Copy to:
           The Honorable _____
           Ranking Minority Member

---

3. <u>Date Line</u>. Do not type the date on correspondence to be signed. Correspondence will be dated by SECNAV Admin once the signature has been obtained.

4. <u>Complimentary Closing</u>. Use "Sincerely," followed by comma for the complimentary close for routine and congressional correspondence. Start the complimentary close at the center of the page on the second line below the text. Also use "Sincerely," for complimentary close of a flag personal letter.

5. <u>Page Numbering</u>. Number second and succeeding pages at the bottom center of the page allowing at least a double space below the last line of text and 1/2 inch from the bottom of the page.

6.   Congressional Committees or Subcommittees Correspondence. Responses addressed to chairpersons of Congressional committees or subcommittees are of particular importance and require additional guidance. Address the response to the chairperson with a courtesy copy to the ranking minority member. The closing paragraph will specify other chairpersons receiving a similar response. Examples of acceptable closing paragraphs are provided in this chapter. SECNAV will sign all correspondence addressed to the chairpersons of Congressional committees or subcommittees except for routine reports to Congress. Correspondence addressing significant or high profile issues will also be signed by SECNAV. Deviation from this policy must be requested and approved through the CLO.

12-4. **General Guidelines for Preparing a Memorandum**. Use memoranda for correspondence within the Office of the Secretary of the Navy, DoD, the President and the White House staff, and to send routine material to other Federal agencies. Standard memorandums are used for routine correspondence within the DON.

1.   Action or Information ("Info") Memorandum

a.   The following procedures shall be used for the preparation of SECNAV action (figure 12-9) or info memorandums (figure 12-10):

(1) Limit to one page, unless issue is complex and requires greater explanation.

(2) Use short, concise and clear bullet statements (use of black dot bullet preferred).

(3) Use 13 point, Times New Roman font.

(4) Page setup: 1-inch margins, top and bottom, right and left.

(5) Double space between headings.

(6) Double space between bullets.

(7) Number pages at bottom center starting on page 2.

(8) If the document is classified, annotate the appropriate security classification markings, with classification/declassified instructions, at the top and bottom of the document.

(9) Do not staple or use clam clips to assemble.

(10) An acronym may be used after it is spelled out the first time.

b.   Lead offices must also prepare an action memo for the following types of correspondence:

(1) Prepare reply for Secretary of Defense (SECDEF) signature (PRS).

(2) Prepare reply for Deputy Secretary of the Defense (DEPSECDEF) signature (PRD).

(3) Answer SECDEF note (ASN).

(4) Answer DEPSECDEF note (ADN).

(5) Answer military assistant note (AMAN).

(6) An action memo signed by a principal or deputy of the lead office must be prepared for submission to the SECDEF, DEPSECDEF via SECNAV and UNSECNAV.

2. Package Assembly

a. The lead office will submit the proposed response to SECNAV Admin after assembling the package for signature. The package will include an action memo or info memo and be set up as follows:

(1) An action or info memo is required when forwarding documents to SECNAV. The action/info memo shall be the top page on the right side of the package.

(2) All tabs must be identified in the action/info memo and shall be placed on the right side of the folder under the memo. Use the following procedures to identify the contents of each tab.

(a) TAB A. The action item (e.g., item for signature or approval). If a similar letter is going to multiple addresses, all letters can go at TAB A. If there are different items for signature or approval, they should be separated at TAB A-1, A-2, etc.

(b) TAB B. Incoming correspondence (if applicable).

(c) TAB C. Background information. If more than one tab is needed, tab accordingly. If substantive or lengthy background information is forwarded, provide a one-page executive summary of the information.

(d) TAB D (or last tab in package). Coordination information. Provide the SECNAV a coordination page to identify a list of coordinating offices/activities (figure 12-11). All coordination shall be provided or listed on one page and should be the last tab. Include office/department, point of contact, phone number and date the package was processed or coordinated. Concurrences must be obtained from heads of the SECNAV components involved, or, in their absence, the principal deputy. List non-concurrence and provide comments at the coordination tab. If the package did not require coordination, state "none" on the action or info memo. When providing coordination, list principles, deputies or executive assistants as points of contact for all correspondence to be signed by the SECNAV or UNSECNAV. Approval/credibility of an action memo often depends on the coordination efforts.

b. Folder Assembly

(1) The package shall be assembled as follows:

Left side
Route Slip/Buck Slip
Incoming Letter
Drafts

Right Side
Action or Info Memo
TAB A (action)
TAB B (reference)
TAB C (summary/chops)
TAB D (coordination)

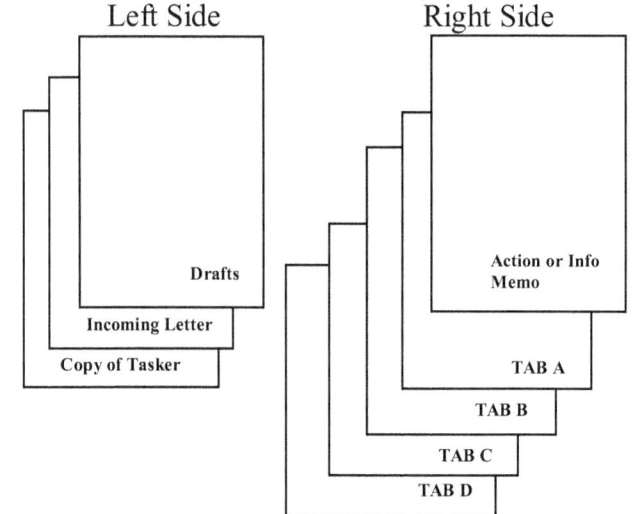

(2) Tabs are required to be typed and displayed in consecutive order on the far right hand side on a separate plain tab paper. The reviewer should be able to see all tabs at once.

SECRETARY OF DEFENSE CORRESPONDENCE ACTION REPORT

Complete this form and forward to WHS/ESD/Correspondence Control Division, Attention: Suspense Desk, Pentagon Room 3C843, Phone (703) 697-9287, Fax (703) 693-7028, Email: SuspenseDesk@whs.mil. Classified Email: suspensedesk@whs.pentagon.smil.mil	TASKED AGENCY
	SUSPENSE DATE *(MMDDYYYY)*

1. REQUESTED ACTION

☐ a. ACTION COMPLETED ☐ COPY ATTACHED and/or ☐ SEE JUSTIFICATION BELOW

☐ b. REQUEST EXTENSION OF SUSPENSE DATE *(MMDDYYYY)* TO _____ *(Justify below)*

☐ c. INTERIM REPLY SENT *(Attach copy)*; EXTEND SUSPENSE DATE *(MMDDYYYY)* TO _____ *(Justify below)*

☐ d. REQUEST CANCELLATION *(Justify below)*

☐ e. REQUEST TRANSFER TO _____ *(Justify below, include POC name and telephone number)*

☐ f. REQUEST DOWNGRADE TO _____ *(Justify below)*

2. JUSTIFICATION

3. TASKED AGENCY

a. AGENCY NAME	b. ACTION OFFICER NAME	c. TELEPHONE NUMBER
d. DATE *(MMDDYYYY)*	e. AGENCY APPROVING AUTHORITY SIGNATURE *(Service Secretary/Under Secretary/ASD Military/ Executive Assistant Level)*	

4. ACTION TAKEN *(For ExecSec/Executive Support Office and Correspondence Control Division Use Only)*

a. ACTION COMPLETED ☐ APPROVED ☐ DISAPPROVED

b. EXTENSION ☐ APPROVED ☐ DISAPPROVED

c. CANCELLATION ☐ APPROVED ☐ DISAPPROVED

d. TRANSFER ☐ APPROVED ☐ DISAPPROVED

e. DOWNGRADE ☐ APPROVED ☐ DISAPPROVED

f. OTHER *(Specify below)* ☐ APPROVED ☐ DISAPPROVED

5. OSD CONTROL NUMBER

g. DATE SIGNED *(MMDDYYYY)*	h. SIGNATURE

SD FORM 391, MAR 2007 PREVIOUS EDITION IS OBSOLETE. [Email] [Print] [Reset] Adobe Designer 7.0

FIGURE 12-1. SD FORM 391– DOD CORRESPONDENCE ACTION REPORT

CHIEF OF NAVAL OPERATIONS
WASHINGTON, DC 20350-1000

April 7, 2009

Mr. or Ms. (   )
1234 Anywhere Street
Everywhere, NV 89701

Dear Mr. or Ms. (   ):

    This is to acknowledge your letter of (April 2, 2007) (Use "recent" letter) to (addressee) concerning (subject). (If not addressed to CNO then insert the following: Your letter has been forwarded to the Chief of Naval Operations for reply). Your letter has been referred to (lead office). I am responding on behalf of (name).

    We are gathering the information necessary to provide you a substantive response and will reply further upon completion of our investigation into this matter. You can expect a final response by (specify date) (up to 30 days from original due date).

    In the interim, if you require further assistance or have additional information to provide, you may contact (name, phone number) who is coordinating the response.

                 Sincerely,

                 G. ROUGHEAD
                 [Title/Position] (Not required when
                         replicated on letterhead)

FIGURE 12-2.   SAMPLE INTERIM RESPONSE FOR INCOMING CORRESPONDENCE

THE SECRETARY OF THE NAVY
WASHINGTON, DC 20350-1000

January 18, 2009

The Honorable (   )
(United States Senate) (House of Representatives)
Washington, DC (20510) (+ (4 digit code)

Dear (Senator or [Mr., Mrs., or Ms.]) (Last Name):

   This is an interim response to your correspondence of (April 2, 2007) (Use "recent" letter if response is not timely) on behalf of your constituent, (Full Name), concerning (Subject).

   We are currently gathering information necessary to provide you a substantive response to address your inquiry. The issue(s) addressed in your letter raised several questions concerning (Subject). You can expect our final reply by (date – December 6, 2005).

   If you should need any further assistance regarding this matter, please contact (Action Officer, E-mail address, and Phone Number).

                              Sincerely,

                              Ray Mabus
                              [Title/Position] (Not required when
                                        replicated on letterhead)

FIGURE 12-3.   SAMPLE INTERIM RESPONSE FOR CONGRESSIONAL
CORRESPONDENCE

DEPARTMENT OF THE NAVY
OFFICE OF THE SECRETARY
1000 NAVY PENTAGON
WASHINGTON, DC 20350-1000

January 15, 2009

The Honorable (Full Name)
Chairman, Committee on
 Armed Services
House of Representatives
Washington, DC 20515

> **Note**: This letterhead should be used only by Principles who are responding on behalf of The Secretary of the Navy and have been directed via Tasker, verbal, or delegation.

Dear Mr. or Madam Chairman:

Thank you for your letter of (July 31, 2007), concerning (Subject), I am responding for the Secretary of the Navy.

(Response).

Again, I appreciate your taking the time to share your thoughts on this issue. If I can be of further assistance, please let me know.

Sincerely,

Sean J. Stackley
Assistant Secretary of the Navy
 (Research, Development and Acquisition)
[Title/Position] (required when not
                              replicated on letterhead)

Enclosure (if applicable)
Note: If a Senator or Congressman/woman uses letterhead paper that lists him/her as Chairperson, the response should be in the above format. Otherwise, address should be:

The Honorable (Full Name)   The Honorable (   )
United States Senate   House of Representatives
Washington, DC 20510   Washington, DC 20515

Dear Senator (Last Name):   Dear Mr., Mrs., Ms.(Last Name):

    A similar letter has been sent to Chairman (   ).
As always, if I can be of further assistance, please let me know.

Copy to:
The Honorable (   )
Ranking Minority Member

FIGURE 12-4.   CONGRESSIONAL RESPONSE, ONE CHAIRPERSON

THE ASSISTANT SECRETARY OF THE NAVY
(RESEARCH, DEVELOPMENT AND ACQUISITION)
1000 NAVY PENTAGON
WASHINGTON, DC 20350-1000

November 29, 2008

The Honorable (Full Name)
Chairman, Committee on
 Armed Services
House of Representatives
Washington, DC 20515

Dear Mr. Chairman:

   Thank you for your letter of (July 31, 2007), concerning (Subject).

   (Response).

   Again, I appreciate your taking the time to share your thoughts on this issue.
If I can be of further assistance, please let me know.

                            Sincerely,

                            Sean J. Stackley
                            [Title/Position] (Not required when
                                      replicated on letterhead)

Enclosure (if applicable)
Note: If a Senator or Congressman/woman uses letterhead paper
that lists him/her as Chairperson, the response should be in the
above format. Otherwise, address should be:

The Honorable (Full Name)   The Honorable (   )
United States Senate   House of Representatives
Washington, DC 20510   Washington, DC 20515

Dear Senator (Last Name):   Dear Mr., Mrs., Ms.(Last Name):

    A similar letter has been sent to Chairman (   ).
As always, if I can be of further assistance, please let me know.

Copy to:
The Honorable (   )
Ranking Minority Member

FIGURE 12-5. CONGRESSIONAL RESPONSE, TWO CHAIRPERSONS

DEPARTMENT OF THE NAVY
OFFICE OF THE SECRETARY
1000 NAVY PENTAGON
WASHINGTON, DC 20350-1000

August 6, 2009

The Honorable (Full Name)
Chairman, Committee on
 Armed Services
House of Representatives
Washington, DC 20515

> **Note**: This letterhead should be used only by Principles who are responding on behalf of The Secretary of the Navy and have been directed via Tasker, verbal, or delegation.

Dear Mr. Chairman:

 Thank you for your letter of (July 31, 2007), concerning (Subject), I am responding for the Secretary of the Navy.

 (Response).

 Again, I appreciate your taking the time to share your thoughts on this issue. If I can be of further assistance, please let me know.

Sincerely,

Robert O. Work
Under Secretary of the Navy
[Title/Position] (Not required when
                                        replicated on letterhead)

Enclosure (if applicable)
Note: If a Senator or Congressman/woman uses letterhead paper that lists him/her as Chairperson, the response should be in the above format. Otherwise, address should be:

The Honorable (Full Name)   The Honorable (   )
United States Senate   House of Representatives
Washington, DC 20510   Washington, DC 20515

Dear Senator (Last Name):   Dear Mr., Mrs., Ms.(Last Name):

 A similar letter has been sent to Chairman (   ). As always, if I can be of further assistance, please let me know.

Copy to:
The Honorable (   )
Ranking Minority Member

FIGURE 12-6. CONGRESSIONAL RESPONSE, TO CHAIRMAN OF A SELECT COMMITTEE

THE SECRETARY OF THE NAVY

12 December 2009

Chief of Naval Operations
2000 Navy Pentagon
Washington, DC 20350-2000

Dear Admiral Roughead,

   Thank you for speaking on my behalf at this year's Navy League
luncheon.

   Your inspiring words received many compliments. Secretary
Gates expressed his appreciation and asked me to pass on many
thanks. I appreciate your valuable time.

   Again, thank you.

Warmest Regards,

Ray Mabus

FIGURE 12-7. FLAG STATIONERY (8 1/2 X 11) – SECRETARY OF THE NAVY

 **CHIEF OF NAVAL OPERATIONS**

Vice Chief of Naval Operations
2000 Navy Pentagon
Washington, DC 20350-2000

Dear Admiral Greenert,

   Thank you for hosting this years speaking on my behalf at this year's Navy League luncheon.

   Your inspiring words received many compliments. Secretary Gates expressed his appreciation and asked me to pass on many thanks. I appreciate your valuable time.

   Again, thank you and I appreciate your valuable time spent and look forward to our next event.

               Sincerely,

               G. ROUGHEAD
               Admiral, U.S. Navy

FIGURE 12-8. FLAG STATIONARY (5 x 7) – CHIEF OF NAVAL OPERATIONS

[USE APPROPRIATE LETTERHEAD]
CLASSIFICATION (if required)

ACTION MEMO

February 21, 2009

FOR: SECRETARY OF THE NAVY

FROM: Anne Brennan, General Counsel of the Navy (Acting) (Full Name, Title)

SUBJECT: Action Memo Format (Use Title Case)

- What the Secretary should do? This bullet explains what action is required. This is different from the entry for recommendation (TAB A).

- Due date for action. This bullet is used for incoming correspondence at TAB B. Do not enter "I would like to have this done by" due date.

- Why it is necessary and/or acceptable for the Secretary to approve or sign the recommended action? This bullet identifies additional key points/contentious issues and any problem areas (TAB C).

RECOMMENDATION: SECNAV approve or sign (TAB A).

> **NOTE**: The recommendation supports the first bullet of the Action Memo. Use this example if there is a document for signature. If no document for proposal/ signature at TAB A use below recommendation:

RECOMMENDATION: That SECNAV release funds by initialing as appropriate:
Approve_____ Disapprove_____

COORDINATION: [TAB D] (or as applicable – last tab) or [None]

ATTACHMENTS:
As stated

Classification/Declassification Authority and Instructions (if required)

Prepared By: Name, Organization, Phone (1 inch from the bottom)

CLASSIFICATION (if required)

FIGURE 12-9. ACTION MEMORANDUM

[USE APPROPRIATE LETTERHEAD]
CLASSIFICATION (if required)

INFO MEMO

December 6, 2009

FOR: SECRETARY OF THE NAVY

FROM: Roger Natsuhara, Assistant Secretary of the Navy (Installations and
         Environment) (Full Name, Title)

SUBJECT: Info Memo Format

Reference: SECNAV M-5216.5

- The first bullet will identify what information is being forwarded and why. If
  forwarding a document, identify as TAB A.

- The second and subsequent bullets will provide additional key points, as required:
  background at TAB A.

- When using a reference line, you would annotate it as shown above. A single
  reference does not get assigned a letter. Multiple references are assigned (a), (b),
  etc. The "R" in reference is the only letter capitalized. You would use the
  reference line like this in all types of Executive Correspondence.

COORDINATION: [TAB D] (or as applicable – last tab) or [None]

ATTACHMENTS:
As stated

**If there is more than one reference the reference line would look like the following:

   References: (a) SECNAV M-5216.5
                (b) SECNAV M-5510.36

Prepared By: Name, Organization, Phone

FIGURE 12-10. INFORMATION MEMORANDUM

[USE PLAIN BOND PAPER]

COORDINATION PAGE

Office/Dept	Point of Contact/Title	Phone	Date
OPNAV (N44)	RDML Jones Director	(703) 555-1212	10 May 09
OPNAV (N4B)	Mrs. A. Whittemore ADCNO	(703) 556-1111	19 Mar 09
DMCS	Col Jones SGS	(703) 697-1668	12 May 09
DNS	VADM Fitzgerald Director	(703) 555-1213	19 Apr 09
ASN I&E	Mr. B.J. Penn ASN	DSN 225-2222	22 May 09
DASN (I&E)	Mr. Wayne Arny DASN	(703) 555-1215	22 May 09

FIGURE 12-11. COORDINATION PAGE

THE SECRETARY OF THE NAVY
WASHINGTON, D.C. 20350-1000

April 7, 2009

MEMORANDUM FOR SECRETARY OF DEFENSE
DEPUTY SECRETARY OF DEFENSE

SUBJECT: Preparing a Memorandum for the Office of the Secretary of Defense

Use memoranda for correspondence within the Department of Defense, to the President and White House staff, and to send routine correspondence to other Federal Agencies. Memos may be sent to multiple addresses, but do not address them to someone through another office or person.

Prepare memos on letterhead appropriate to the signing official. Set a two-inch top margin and one-inch side and bottom margin on first pages. Use plain paper for succeeding pages with one-inch margins on all sides.

Single-space paragraphs and double–space paragraphs between them. Indent paragraphs a half-inch from the left margin. Indent subparagraphs an additional half- inch and identify them with bullets, numbers, and lower case letters. Double space between subparagraphs

Do not date memos the Secretary or Deputy Secretary of Defense will sign. The date shall be added when signed. Also omit the signature line on memos the Secretary or Deputy Secretary of Defense will sign. For other officials, the signature line may be typed or stamped leaving four blank lines below the text, beginning at the center of the page. Run-over lines should be indented two spaces. The title in the signature line may be omitted if the signer's position is reflected in the letterhead.

Normally attachments shall be identified in the text of the memo. When this is the case the notation "Attachments: As stated" shall be typed at the left margin a double space below the signature line. When attachments are not identified, list all of them in the order they appear in the text.

Ray Mabus

Attachments:
As stated

cc:
General Counsel

FIGURE 12-12. STANDARD MEMORANDUM FOR

APPENDIX A

MILITARY MODELS OF ADDRESS

Addressee	Letter and Envelope	Salutation

Navy and Coast Guard Officers

Addressee	Letter and Envelope	Salutation
Admiral	ADM	Dear Admiral (surname):
Vice Admiral	VADM	"
Rear Admiral (Upper Half)	RADM	"
Rear Admiral (Lower Half)	RDML	
Captain	CAPT	Dear Captain (surname):
Commander	CDR	Dear Commander (surname):
Lieutenant Commander	LCDR	"
Lieutenant	LT	Dear Lieutenant (surname):
Lieutenant Junior Grade	LTJG	"
Ensign	ENS	Dear Ensign (surname):
Chief Warrant Officer	CWO5	Dear Chief Warrant Officer (surname):
	CWO4	Dear Chief Warrant Officer (surname):
	CWO3	Dear Chief Warrant Officer (surname):
	CWO2	Dear Chief Warrant Officer (surname):
Warrant Officer	WO	Dear Warrant Officer (surname):

Marine Corps, Air Force, and Army Officers

Addressee	Marines	Air Force	Army	Salutation
General	Gen	Gen	GEN	Dear General (surname):
Lieutenant General	LtGen	Lt Gen	LTG	"
Major General	MajGen	Maj Gen	MG	"
Brigadier General	BGen	Brig Gen	BG	"
Colonel	Col	Col	COL	Dear Colonel (surname):
Lieutenant Colonel	LtCol	Lt Col	LTC	"
Major	Maj	Maj	MAJ	Dear Major (surname):
Captain	Capt	Capt	CPT	Dear Captain (surname):
First Lieutenant	1stLt	1st Lt	1LT	Dear Lieutenant (surname):
Second Lieutenant	2ndLt	2nd Lt	2LT	"
Chief Warrant Officer 5	CWO5		CW5	Dear Chief Warrant Officer (surname):
Chief Warrant Officer 4	CWO4		CW4	"
Chief Warrant Officer 3	CWO3		CW3	"
Chief Warrant Officer 2	CWO2		CW2	"
Warrant Officer	WO		WO1	Dear Warrant Officer (surname):

Navy and Coast Guard Enlisted

Addressee	Letter and Envelope	Salutation
Master Chief Petty Officer of the Navy	MCPON	Dear Master Chief (surname):
Master Chief Petty Officer of the Coast Guard	MCPOCG	"
Master Chief Petty Officer	MCPO	"
Senior Chief Petty Officer	SCPO	Dear Senior Chief (surname):
Chief Petty Officer	CPO	Dear Chief (surname):

Addressee	Letter and Envelope	Salutation
Petty Officer First Class	PO1	Dear Petty Officer (surname):
Petty Officer Second Class	PO2	
Petty Officer Third Class	PO3	
Airman (includes Apprentice and Recruit)	AN or AA or AR	Dear Airman (surname):
Constructionman (includes Apprentice and Recruit)	CN or CA or CR	Dear Constructionman (surname):
Fireman (includes Apprentice and Recruit)	FN or FA or SR	Dear Fireman (surname):
Hospitalman (includes Apprentice and Recruit)	HN or HA or HR	Dear Hospitalman (surname):
Seaman (includes Apprentice and Recruit)	SN or SA or SR	Dear Seaman (surname):

Marine Corps Enlisted

Sergeant Major of the Marine Corps	SgtMaj	Dear Sergeant Major (surname):
Sergeant Major	SgtMaj	"
Master Gunnery Sergeant	MGySgt	Dear Master Gunnery Sergeant (surname):
First Sergeant	lstSgt	Dear First Sergeant (surname):
Master Sergeant	MSgt	Dear Master Sergeant (surname):
Gunnery Sergeant	GySgt	Dear Gunnery Sergeant (surname):
Staff Sergeant	SSgt	Dear Staff Sergeant (surname):
Sergeant	Sgt	Dear Sergeant (surname):
Corporal	Cpl	Dear Corporal (surname):
Lance Corporal	LCpl	"
Private First Class	PFC	Dear Private First Class (surname):
Private	Pvt	Dear Private (surname):

Army Enlisted

Sergeant Major of the Army	SMA	Dear Sergeant Major (surname):
Command Sergeant Major	CSM	"
Sergeant Major	SGM	"
First Sergeant	1SG	Dear First Sergeant (surname):
Master Sergeant	MSG	Dear Master Sergeant (surname):
Platoon Sergeant	PSG	Dear Sergeant (surname):
Sergeant First Class	SFC	"
Staff Sergeant	SSG	"
Sergeant	SGT	"
Corporal	CPL	Dear Corporal (surname):
Private First Class	PFC	Dear Private (surname):
Private	PVT	"
Specialists (all grades)	SP7	Dear Specialist (surname):
	SP6	"
	(etc)	

A-2

Addressee	Letter and Envelope	Salutation

Air Force Enlisted

Addressee	Letter and Envelope	Salutation
Chief Master Sergeant of the Air Force	CMSAF	Dear Chief (surname):
Chief Master Sergeant	CMSgt	"
Senior Master Sergeant	SMSgt	Dear Sergeant (surname):
Master Sergeant	MSgt	"
Technical Sergeant	TSgt	"
Staff Sergeant	SSgt	"
Sergeant	Sgt	"
Senior Airman	SrA	Dear Airman (surname):
Airman First Class	A1C	"
Airman	Azun	"
Airman Basic	AB	"

Other Military

Addressee	Letter and Envelope	Salutation
All retired military	(rank) (full name), (USN, USMCR or other branch) (Ret)	Dear (rank) (surname):
Chaplain	Chaplain (full name) (rank), CHC, USN	Dear Chaplain (surname):

APPENDIX B

CIVILIAN MODELS OF ADDRESS

1. The following examples of civilian models of address, salutation, and complimentary close are used in the preparation of Navy business-format letters. They may be varied depending on circumstances.

2. Use "The Honorable (Name)" in the address of Presidential appointees as well as Federal and state elected officials. Avoid "The Honorable" in addresses of county and city officials, except for mayors.

3. Use the title "Madam" in the salutation of a letter to a high-level woman diplomat or government official, such as the United States Ambassador to the United Nations. Use the title "Madam" in salutations of letters destined for women foreign heads of state and diplomats.

4. Use the title "Ms." when addressing a woman by her surname (Ms. Jones). However, "Ms.," like "Mr.," indicates nothing with regard to a person's marital status. Therefore, use "Miss" or "Mrs." in the salutation when an incumbent or correspondent has indicated this preference. Never use "Ms." with a woman's full married name; e.g., "Ms. John E. Doe" is incorrect. Use "Mr." with a position or surname if you don't know the addressee's gender and can't find out readily.

MODELS OF ADDRESS AND SALUTATION

Addressee	Letter and Envelope	Salutation and Complimentary Close
The White House		
The President	The President The White House Washington, DC 20500-0001	Dear Mr. (or Madam) President: Respectfully yours,
Husband (or Wife) of the President	Mr. (or Ms.) (full name) The White House Washington, DC 20500-0001	Dear Mr. (or Ms.) (surname): Sincerely,
Assistant to the President	The Honorable (full name) Assistant to the President The White House Washington, DC 20500-000 1	Dear Mr. (or Ms.) (surname): Sincerely,
Secretary to the President	The Honorable (full name) Secretary to the President The White House Washington, DC 20500-0001	Dear Mr. (or Ms.) (surname): Sincerely,
Secretary to the President (with military rank)	(full rank) (full name) Secretary to the President The White House Washington, DC 20500-0001	Dear (rank) (surname): Sincerely,
The Vice President		
As Vice President	The Vice President The White House Washington, DC 20500-0001	Dear Mr. (or Madam) Vice President: Sincerely,
As Senate President	The Honorable (full name) President of the Senate Washington, DC 20510-0001	Dear Mr. (or Madam) President: Sincerely,
The Judiciary		
The Chief Justice	The Chief Justice of the United States The Supreme Court of the United States Washington, DC 20543-0001	Dear Mr. (or Madam) Chief Justice: Sincerely,
Associate Justice	Mr. (or Madam) Justice (surname) The Supreme Court of the United States Washington, DC 20543-0001	Dear Mr. (or Madam) Justice: Sincerely,
Retired Justice	The Honorable (full name) (local address)	Dear Mr. (or Madam) Justice: Sincerely,
Presiding Justice	The Honorable (full name) Presiding Justice (name of the court) (local address)	Dear Mr. (or Madam) Justice: Sincerely,

Judge of a Court	The Honorable (full name)
	Judge of the (name of court;
	  if a U.S. district court,
	  give district).
	(local address)
		Dear Judge (surname):
		Sincerely,

Addressee	Letter and Envelope	Salutation and Complimentary Close
Clerk of a Court	Mr. (or Ms.) (full name) Clerk of the (name of court; if a U.S. district court, give district). (local address)	Dear Mr. (or Ms.) (surname): Sincerely,
Attorney	Mr. (or Ms.) (full name) Attorney at Law (local address)	Dear Mr. (or Ms.) (surname): Sincerely,

The Senate

Addressee	Letter and Envelope	Salutation and Complimentary Close

President pro Tempore
  of the Senate
	The Honorable (full name)
	President pro Tempore
	  of the Senate
	United States Senate
	Washington, DC 20510-0000
		Dear Senator (surname):
		Sincerely,

Committee Chairman,
  U.S. Senate
	The Honorable (full name)
	Chairman, Committee on
	  (name of committee)
	United States Senate
	Washington, DC 20510-0000
		Dear Mr. (or Madam)
		Sincerely,

Subcommittee Chairman
  U. S. Senate
	The Honorable (full name)
	Chairman, Subcommittee on
	  (name of subcommittee)
	(name of parent committee)
	United States Senate
	Washington, DC 20510-0000
		Dear Senator (surname):
		Sincerely,
		OR
		Dear Mr. (or Madam) Chairman:
		Sincerely,
		(When incoming correspondence
		is so signed and pertains to
		subcommittee business)

United States Senator (Washington, DC office)	The Honorable (full name) United States Senate Washington, DC 20510-0000 OR	Dear Senator (surname): Sincerely,
(Away from Washington, DC)	The Honorable (full name) United States Senator (local address)	Dear Senator (surname): Sincerely,

Senator, Majority (or Minority)
  Leader
  (Washington, DC office)
	The Honorable (full name)
	Majority (or Minority) Leader
	United States Senate
	Washington, DC 20510-0000
	OR
		Dear Senator (surname):
		Sincerely,

(Away from Washington, DC)	The Honorable (full name) Majority (or Minority) Leader United States Senate (local address)	Dear Senator (surname): Sincerely,
United States Senator-elect (Washington, DC office)	The Honorable (full name) United States Senator-elect United States Senate Washington, DC 20510-0000 OR	Dear Mr. (or Ms.) (surname): Sincerely,
(Away from Washington, DC)	Mr. (or Ms.) (full name) United States Senator-elect (local address, if given)	Dear Mr. (or Ms.) (surname): Sincerely,

B-3

Addressee	Letter and Envelope	Salutation and Complimentary Close
Office of a deceased Senator	Mr. (or Ms.) (Secretary's full name, if known) Secretary to the Late Honorable (full name) United States Senate Washington, DC 20510-0000	Dear Mr. (or Ms.) (surname): Sincerely,
Former Senator	The Honorable (full name) (local address)	Dear Senator (surname): Sincerely,
Secretary of the Senate	The Honorable (full name) Secretary of the Senate Washington, DC 20510-0000	Dear Mr. (or Ms.) (surname): Sincerely,
Secretary or Administrative Assistant to a Senator	Mr. (or Ms.) (full name) Secretary/Administrative Assistant to the Honorable (full name) United States Senate Washington, DC 20510-0000	Dear Mr. (or Ms.) (surname): Sincerely,

House of Representatives

Addressee	Letter and Envelope	Salutation and Complimentary Close
Speaker of the House of Representatives	The Honorable (full name) Speaker of the House of Representatives Washington, DC 20515-0000	Dear Mr. (or Madam) Speaker: Sincerely,
Committee Chairman	The Honorable (full name) Chairman, Committee on (name of committee) House of Representatives Washington, DC 20515-0000	Dear Mr. (or Madam) Chairman: Sincerely,
Subcommittee Chairman	The Honorable (full name) Chairman, Subcommittee on (name of subcommittee) (Name of parent committee) House of Representatives Washington, DC 20515-0000	Dear Mr. (or Ms.) (surname): Sincerely, OR Dear Mr. (or Madam) Chairman: Sincerely, (When incoming correspondence is so signed and pertains to subcommittee business)
United States Representative (Washington, DC office)	The Honorable (full name) House of Representatives Washington, DC 20515-0000 OR	Dear Mr. (or Ms.) (surname): Sincerely,
(Away from Washington, DC)	The Honorable (full name) Member, United States House of Representatives (local address)	Dear Mr. (or Ms.) (surname): Sincerely,
Representative-elect	The Honorable (full name) Representative-elect House of Representatives Washington, DC 20515-0000 OR Mr. (or Ms.) (full name) Representative-elect (local address, if given)	Dear Mr. (or Ms.) (surname): Sincerely, Dear Mr. (or Ms.) (surname): Sincerely,

Addressee	Letter and Envelope	Salutation and Complimentary Close
Office of a deceased Representative	Mr. (or Ms.) (Secretary's full name, if known) Secretary to the Late Honorable (full name) House of Representatives Washington, DC 20515-0000	Dear Mr. (or Ms.) (surname): Sincerely,
Former Representative	The Honorable (full name) (local address)	Dear Mr. (or Ms.) (surname): Sincerely,
Resident Commissioner	The Honorable (full name) Resident Commissioner from (name of area) House of Representatives Washington, DC 20515-0000	Dear Mr. (or Ms.) (surname): Sincerely,
Delegate of the District of Columbia	The Honorable (full name) House of Representatives Washington, DC 20515-0000	Dear Mr. (or Ms.) (surname): Sincerely,

Legislative Agencies

Comptroller General (Head of the General Accounting Office)	The Honorable (full name) Comptroller General of the United States Washington, DC 20548-0000	Dear Mr. (or Ms.) (surname): Sincerely,
Public Printer (Head of the U.S. Government Printing Office)	The Honorable (full name) U.S. Government Printing Office Washington, DC 20401-0000	Dear Mr. (or Ms.) (surname): Sincerely,
Librarian of Congress	The Honorable (full name) Librarian of Congress Washington, DC 20540-0000	Dear Mr. (or Ms.) (surname): Sincerely,

Executive Departments

Members of the Cabinet (if addressed as 'Secretary")	The Honorable (full name) Secretary of (name of department)* Washington, DC 00000-0000	Dear Mr. (or Madam) Secretary: Sincerely,
Attorney General (Head of the Department of Justice	The Honorable (full name) Attorney General Washington, DC 00000-0000	Dear Mr. (or Madam) Attorney General Sincerely,
Under Secretary of a Department	The Honorable (full name) Under Secretary of (name of department) Washington, DC 00000-0000	Dear Mr. (or Ms.) (surname): Sincerely,
Deputy Secretary of a Department	The Honorable (full name) Deputy Secretary of (name of department) Washington, DC 00000-0000	Dear Mr. (or Ms.) (surname): Sincerely,
Assistant Secretary of a Department	The Honorable (full name) Assistant Secretary of (name of department) Washington, DC 00000-0000	Dear Mr. (or Ms.) (surname): Sincerely,

*Titles for Cabinet Secretaries are: Secretary of Agriculture, Secretary of Commerce, Secretary of Defense, Secretary of Education, Secretary of Energy, Secretary of Health and Human Services, Secretary of Housing and Urban Development, Secretary of Interior, Secretary of Labor, Secretary of State, Secretary of Transportation, and Secretary of the Treasury.

Addressee	Letter and Envelope	Salutation and Complimentary Close
Independent Organizations		
Director, Office of Management and Budget	Honorable (full name) Director, Office of Management and Budget Washington, DC 20503-0000	Dear Mr. (or Ms.) (surname): Sincerely,
Head of a Federal Agency,	The Honorable (full name) (title), (name of agency) Washington, DC 00000-0000	Dear Mr. (or Ms.) (surname): Sincerely,
Head of a major organization within an agency (if appointed by the President)	The Honorable (full name) (title) (organization) (name of agency) Washington, DC 00000-0000	Dear Mr. (or Ms.) (surname): Sincerely,
President of a Commission	The Honorable (full name) President, (name of commission) Washington, DC 00000-0000	Dear Mr. (or Ms.) (surname): Sincerely,
Chairman of a Commission	The Honorable (full name) Chairman, (name of commission) Washington, DC 00000-0000	Dear Mr. (or Madam) Chairman: Sincerely,
Chairman of a Board	The Honorable (full name) Chairman, (name of board) Washington, DC 00000-0000	Dear Mr. (or Madam) Chairman: Sincerely,
Postmaster General	The Honorable (full name) Postmaster General Washington, DC 00000-0000	Dear Mr. (or Madam) Postmaster General Sincerely,
American Missions		
American Ambassador	The Honorable (full name) American Ambassador American Embassy (city), (country)	Sir (or Madam): (formal) Dear Mr. (or Madam) Ambassador: (informal) Sincerely,
American Ambassador (with military rank)	(full rank) (full name) American Ambassador American Embassy (city), (country)	Sir (or Madam): (formal) Dear (rank) (surname): (informal) Sincerely,
American Minister	The Honorable (full name) American Minister (city), (country)	Sir (or Madam): (formal) Dear Mr. (or Madam) Minister: (informal) Sincerely,
American Minister (with military rank)	(full rank) (full name) American Minister (city), (country)	Sir (or Madam): (formal) Dear (rank) (surname): (informal) Sincerely,

Addressee	Letter and Envelope	Salutation and Complimentary Close
Foreign Government Officials		
Foreign Ambassador in the United States	His (or Her) Excellency (full name) Ambassador of (country) (local address) 00000-0000	Excellency: (formal) Dear Mr. (or Madam) Ambassador: (informal) Sincerely,
Foreign Minister in the United States	The Honorable (full name) Minister of (country) (local address) 00000-0000	Sir (or Madam): (formal) Dear Mr. (or Madam) Minister: (informal) Sincerely,
Foreign Charge d'Affaires in the United States	Mr. (or Madam) (full name) Charge d'Affaires of (country) (local address) 00000-0000	Sir (or Madam): (formal) Dear Mr. (or Madam) Charge Affaires: (informal) Sincerely,
State and Local Government		
Governor of State	The Honorable (full name) Governor of (state) (city), (state) 00000-0000	Dear Governor (surname): Sincerely,
Acting Governor of a State	The Honorable (full name) Acting Governor of (state) (city), (state) 00000-0000	Dear Mr. (or Ms.) (surname): Sincerely,
Lieutenant Governor of a State	The Honorable (full name) Lieutenant Governor of (state) (city), (state) 00000-0000	Dear Governor (surname): Sincerely,
Secretary of state of a State	The Honorable (full name) Secretary of state of (state) (city), (state) 00000-0000	Dear Mr. (or Ms.) (surname): Sincerely,
Chief Justice of the Supreme Court of a State	The Honorable (full name) Chief Justice of the Supreme Court of the State of (state) (city), (state) 00000-0000	Dear Mr. (or Madam) Chief Justice: Sincerely,
Attorney General of a State	The Honorable (full name) Attorney General of the State of (state) (city), (state) 00000-0000	Dear Mr. (or Madam) Attorney General Sincerely,
Treasurer, Comptroller, or Auditor of a State	The Honorable (full name) State Treasurer (Comptroller or Auditor) of the State of (state) (city), (state) 00000-0000	Dear Mr. (or Ms.) (surname): Sincerely,
President of the Senate of a State	The Honorable (full name) President of the Senate of the State of (state) (city), (state) 00000-0000	Dear Mr. (or Ms.) (surname): Sincerely,

Addressee	Letter and Envelope	Salutation and Complimentary Close
State Senator	The Honorable (full name) (state) Senate (city), (state) 00000-0000	Dear Mr. (or Ms.) (surname): Sincerely,
State Representative, Assemblyman or Delegate	The Honorable (full name) (state) House of Representatives (Assembly or House of Delegates) (city), (state) 00000-0000	Dear Mr. (or Ms.) (surname): Sincerely,
Mayor	The Honorable (full name) Mayor of (city) (city), (state) 00000-0000	Dear Mayor (surname): Sincerely,

Ecclesiastical Organizations

Roman Catholic Church

Addressee	Letter and Envelope	Salutation and Complimentary Close
Cardinal	His Eminence (Christian name) Cardinal (surname) Archbishop of (Archdiocese) (local address) 00000-0000	Your Eminence: (formal) Dear Cardinal (surname): (informal) Sincerely,
Archbishop	The Most Reverend (full name) Archbishop of (Archdiocese) (local address) 00000-0000	Your Excellency: (formal) Dear Archbishop (surname): (informal) Sincerely
Bishop	The Most Reverend (full name) Bishop of (diocese) (local address) 00000-0000	Your Excellency: (formal) Dear Bishop (surname): (informal) Sincerely,
Monsignor	The Reverend Monsignor (full name) (local address) 00000-0000 (informal)	Reverend Monsignor: (formal) Dear Monsignor (surname): Sincerely,
Priest	The Reverend (full name) (initials of the order, if any, after name) (local address) 00000-0000	Reverend Father: (formal) Dear Father (surname): (informal) Sincerely,
Superior of a Sisterhood	The Reverend Mother Superior (name of institution) (local address) 00000-0000 (informal)	Dear Reverend Mother: (formal) Dear Mother (name): Sincerely,
Sister	Sister (full name) (name of organization) (local address) 00000-0000	Dear Sister (full name): Sincerely,
Superior of a Brotherhood	Brother (name) Superior of (institution) (local address) 00000-0000	Dear Brother: Sincerely,
Member of a Brotherhood	Brother (full name) (name of organization) (local address) 00000-0000	Dear Brother (full name): Sincerely,

Addressee	Letter and Envelope	Salutation and Complimentary Close
Anglican/Episcopal Church		
Bishop	The Right Reverend (full name) (local address) 00000-0000 (informal)	Right Reverend: (formal) Dear Bishop (surname): Sincerely,
Archdeacon	The Venerable (full name) Archdeacon of (name) (local address) 00000-0000	Venerable Sir (or Madam): (formal) Dear Archdeacon (surname): (informal) Sincerely,
Dean	The Very Reverend (full name) Dean of (church) (local address) 00000-0000	Very Reverend: (formal) Dear Dean (surname): (informal) Sincerely,
Canon	The Very Reverend (full name) Canon of (church) (local address) 00000-0000	Very Reverend: (formal) Dear Canon (surname): (informal) Sincerely,
Rector	The Reverend (full name) The Rector of (name) (local address) 00000-0000	Reverend: (formal) Dear (Dr., Mr., or Ms.) (surname): (informal) Sincerely,
Clergy of Other Denominations		
Methodist Bishop	The Reverend (full name) Methodist Bishop (local address) 00000-0000	Reverend: (formal) Dear Bishop (surname): (informal) Sincerely,
Mormon Elder	Elder (or Brother) (full name) Church of Jesus Christ of Latter Day Saints (local address) 00000-0000	Dear Elder (surname): Sincerely,
Presbyterian Moderator	The Moderator of (name) (local address) 00000-0000 OR The Reverend (full name) Moderator of (name) (local address) 00000-0000	Dear Reverend: (formal) Dear (Dr., Mr., or Ms.) (surname): (informal) Sincerely,
Rabbi	Rabbi (full name) (local address) 00000-0000	Dear Rabbi (surname): Sincerely,
Seventh-Day Adventist Elder	Elder (full name) General Conference of Seventh-day Adventists (local address) 00000-0000	Dear Elder (surname): Sincerely,
Minister, Pastor or Rector (with doctorate)	The Reverend (full name) (title, name of church) (local address) 00000-0000	Dear Dr. (surname): Sincerely,

Addressee	Letter and Envelope	Salutation and Complimentary Close
Minister, Pastor or Rector (without doctorate)	The Reverend (full name) (title, name of church) (local address) 00000-0000	Dear Reverend: (surname):
Eastern Orthodox Archbishop/ Metropolitan	His Eminence (Christian Name) Archbishop of (city) (local address) 00000-0000	Your Eminence: (formal) Dear Archbishop (surname) Sincerely,
Eastern Orthodox Bishop	The Right Reverend (Christian name) Bishop of (city) (local address) 00000-0000	Your Grace: (formal) Dear Bishop: (informal) Sincerely,
Eastern Orthodox Priest	The Reverend (name) (local address) 00000-0000	Dear Reverend Father: (formal) Dear Father (Christian name): (informal) Sincerely,

Educational Institutions

Addressee	Letter and Envelope	Salutation and Complimentary Close
President of a College or University	Dr. (full name) President, (name of institution) (local address) 00000-0000	Dear Dr. (surname): Sincerely,
Dean of a University or College	Dean (full name) School of (name) (name of institution) (local address) 00000-0000	Dear Dr. (surname): ("Dear Dean" if without doctoral degree) Sincerely,
Professor	Professor (full name) Department of (name) (name of institution) (local address) 00000-0000	Dear Dr. (surname): ("Dear Professor" if without doctoral degree) Sincerely,

Other Addressees

Addressee	Letter and Envelope	Salutation and Complimentary Close
An Unmarried Woman	Ms. (or Miss) (full name) (local address) 00000 -0000	Dear Ms. (or Miss) (surname): Sincerely,
A Married Woman or Widow	Ms. (or Mrs.) (husband's full name) (local address) 00000-0000	Dear Ms. (or Mrs.) (surname): Sincerely,
Two or More Unmarried Women	Mses. (surname) and (surname) (local address) 00000-0000 Ms. (or Miss) (full name) and Ms. (or Miss) (full name) (local address) 00000-0000	Ladies (or Mesdames): OR Dear Msess. (or Misses) OR (surname) and (surname): Sincerely,
Two or More Men	Messrs. (surname) and (surname) (local address) 0000-0000 OR Mr. (full name) and Mr. (full name) (local address) 00000-0000	Gentlemen: OR Dear Mr. (surname) and Mr. (surname): Sincerely,

APPENDIX C

STATIONERY REQUIREMENTS

1. <u>Preprinted Letterhead</u>

a. <u>Printing</u>. Preprinted letterhead may be produced by letterpress, or offset lithography, whichever is more economical. Embossing or engraving processes, including thermographic processes are prohibited unless approved by the local Document Automation and Production Service (DAPS).

b. <u>Seal</u>. All "official" letterhead stationery of the DON shall bear a 1-inch diameter of the DoD seal 1/2 inch from the upper left and top edge of the sheet.

c. <u>Other Emblematic Devices</u>. Other seals, emblems, insignia, decorative, or emblematic devices shall not be incorporated.

d. <u>Preprinted Letterhead Language, Typography, and Printing</u>. All components of the DON and Headquarters United States Marine Corps shall comply with the following. (Other Marine Corps activities refer to Marine Corps Publications and Printing Regulations, MCO P5600.31G).

(1) <u>First Line</u>. DEPARTMENT OF THE NAVY centered horizontally 5/8 of an inch from the top edge of the sheet in 10 to 12 point type. Try to match the following font styles: Copperplate BT, Copperplate 32, Univers 55 (Roman) or Helvetica Roman.

(2) <u>Individual Activity Name</u>. Six to nine point matching font.

(3) <u>Address and Zone Improvement Plan (Zip) Code</u>. Six-point capital letters. Center horizontally. Do not use building numbers as part of the zip code, i.e. 17055-0791.

(4) <u>Leading</u>. (space between lines) should be 13 points.

(5) <u>Spacing</u>. The bottom of the printing shall be 1 and 1/16 inch from the top of the trimmed sheet.

(6) <u>Color of Ink</u>. Blue, Pantone Matching system (PMS) 288 or equivalent. Black ink is an acceptable substitute but shall not be used for letterhead to be signed by the senior officials identified in the following paragraph.

(7) <u>Paper Stock</u>. Letterhead stationery and continuation sheets for the SECDEF or DEPSECDEF; the SECNAV, Deputy Secretary, UNSECNAV, and ASNs; the CNO and VCNO; and the CMC and ACMC are not to exceed 20-pound basis weight (per 1000 sheets) 100 percent white bond, JCP G80; all other official letterhead stationery is not to exceed 20-pound basis weight (per 1000 sheets) 25 percent white bond, JCP G40.

(8) <u>Trim Size</u>. Eight and half inches by eleven inches.

2. <u>Computer Generated Letterhead</u> is an acceptable substitute for preprinted letterhead. The format standards and specifications for preprinted letterhead shall be applied to computer generated letterhead to the extent practicable. Digital or electronic signatures may be used to sign computer generated letterhead. Adhere to the DON Chief Information Office guidance for use of digital and/or electronic signatures (refer to paragraph 6 of chapter 4). The following font and format guidance will assist in maintaining professional looking letterhead within the DON.

    a. <u>Font</u>. Recommended fonts for computer generated letterhead are **Times New Roman**, **Century Schoolbook**, `Courier New`, **Helvetica** or **Univers** (10 point bold for the DEPARTMENT OF THE NAVY line and 8 point for the address lines). Try to match the layouts shown.

    b. <u>Spacing</u>. The first line of the letterhead shall be centered on the fourth line from the top of the page.

3. <u>Optional Features</u>

    a. The phrase IN REPLY REFER TO may be printed in 5 point capital letters.

    b. Marking to indicate address area for window envelopes.

    c. Fold markings to indicate business letter folds.

    d. A 1/2 point rule, 1 1/2 picas (approximately 3/4 inch long) placed 1 1/2 inches from the bottom.

    e. Slogans, when approved by the Office of the Secretary of the Navy, printed in the bottom margin approximately 1/2 inch from the bottom of the page.

4. <u>Letterhead Envelopes and Mailing Labels</u> shall conform to USPS standards and OPNAVINST 5218.7B.

    a. <u>First Line</u>. Navy activities and Headquarters, Marine Cops shall print DEPARTMENT OF THE NAVY horizontally 3/8 inch from the top margin in 10 point capital letters. (Other Marine Corps activities refer to MCO P5600.31G).

    b. <u>Individual Activity Name</u>. Use 6 point capital letters.

    c. <u>Official Business</u>. OFFICIAL BUSINESS is printed two lines below the last line of the address text in 6 point capital letters.

    d. <u>Ancillary Services Endorsement</u>. Endorsements such as "Forwarding Service Requested" or "Return Service Requested" are optional. When added to the envelope or label it should be placed two lines below the OFFICIAL BUSINESS phrase in 6 point capital letters.

e. <u>Leading</u>. Should be 13 points between each line. Center 3 pica hairline rules 6 points apart under DEPARTMENT OF THE NAVY and above OFFICIAL BUSINESS.

f. <u>Borders, Markings, Slogans, or Designs</u>. Shall not be imprinted or affixed.

g. <u>Labels</u>. Label size shall be no smaller than 5 inches by 3 inches. Margins for marginally punched labels may be adjusted as required to allow necessary edge punching.

h. <u>Colors ofInk</u>. Labels shall be printed in black. Envelopes shall be printed in either black or blue (PMS 288 or equivalent).

DEPARTMENT OF THE NAVY
OFFICE OF THE SECRETARY
1000 NAVY PENTAGON
WASHINGTON, DC 20350-1000

DEPARTMENT OF THE NAVY
OFFICE OF THE CHIEF OF NAVAL OPERATIONS
2000 NAVY PENTAGON
WASHINGTON, DC 20350-2000

IN REPLY REFER TO

DEPARTMENT OF THE NAVY
HEADQUARTERS, UNITED STATES MARINE CORPS
3000 MARINE CORPS PENTAGON
WASHINGTON, DC 20380-1775

UNITED STATES MARINE CORPS
COMMUNICATIONS COMPANY
HEADQUARTERS BATTALION
CAMP PENDLETON, CA 92055-5006

APPENDIX D

FORMS AND ENVELOPES

1. The following forms are available for download from GSA Forms Web site:
http://www.gsa.gov/Portal/gsa/ep/formsWelcome.do?pageTypeId=8199&channelId=-25201:

FORM	STOCK NUMBER	UI	QTY
OF 363 Memorandum of Call	PDF Format		

2. The following forms are available from Naval Forms Online (NFOL):
https://navalforms.daps.dla.mil/web/public/home:

FORM	STOCK NUMBER	UI	QTY
OPNAV 5211/7 (Rev: Jun 1981) Correspondence/Documents Control Card	0107-LF-052-1137	PG	100
OPNAV 5216/144A (Rev: Aug 1981) DON Memo (8-1/2 x 11)	PDF Format		
OPNAV 5216/144B (Rev: Aug 1981) DON Memo (8-1/2 x 5-1/2)	PDF Format		
OPNAV 5216/158 (Rev: Jul 1978) Routine Reply, Endorsement Transmittal or Information Sheet	PDF Format		

3. The following forms are available for purchase from GSA Global Supply: http://www.gsa.gov/glovalsupply or (800)525-8027, option 3:

FORM	STOCK NUMBER	UI	QTY
OF 65A U.S. Government Messenger Envelope (Large, 4-1/8 x 9-1/2)	7540-00-117-8424	BX	200
OF 65B U.S. Government Messenger Envelope (Medium. 9-1/2 x 12)	7540-00-222-3467	BX	250
OF 65C U.S. Government Messenger Envelope (Small, 12 x 16)	7540-00-222-3468	BX	250
OF 99 Fax Transmittal	7540-01-317-7368	PD	50

4. The following envelopes are available from GSA:

ENVELOPE	STYLE NO.	UI	QTY
Plain, white #10 (4-1/8 x 9-1/2)	192	BX	500
Plain, brown (8-1/2 x 11-1/2)	68	BX	500
Plain, brown (12 x 9-1/2)	84	BX	500
Plain, brown (16 x 12)	104	BX	500

APPENDIX E
INDEX

THIS PAGE INTENTIONALLY LEFT BLANK

SECNAV M-5216.5

Stock Number
0516LP1100043